The Urbana Free Library

To renew: call 217-367-4057
or go to *"urbanafreelibrary.org"*
and select "Renew/Request Items"

Coffee Talk

Coffee Talk

The Stimulating Story of the World's Most Popular Brew

Morton Satin

Prometheus Books

59 John Glenn Drive
Amherst, New York 14228–2119

Published 2011 by Prometheus Books

Inquiries should be addressed to
Prometheus Books
59 John Glenn Drive
Amherst, New York 14228–2119
VOICE: 716–691–0133
FAX: 716–691–0137
WWW.PROMETHEUSBOOKS.COM

15 14 13 12 11   5 4 3 2 1

Library of Congress Cataloging-in-Publication Data

Satin, Morton.
    Coffee talk : the stimulating story of the world's most popular brew / by Morton Satin.
        p. cm.
    Includes bibliographical references and index.
    ISBN 978–1–59102–688–4 (hardcover : alk. paper)
    1. Coffee. 2. Coffeehouses. I. Title.

TX415.S27 2009
641.3'373—dc22

2008049255

For Miriam

Contents

PART 2: COFFEE'S PLACE IN CULTURE AND ECONOMIC DEVELOPMENT

PART 3: COFFEE'S RENAISSANCE IN A NEW WORLD

Preface

"Watch carefully, just a little pinch of salt, that's all," my father quietly told me as I looked on from my perch on the wooden milk crate. I was all of seven at the time and was spending my summer helping my father in his flea-sized snack stand in Montréal's garment district. The walls of several buildings still had remnants of the joyous graffiti painted on a few years back, "No More War!!" referring to the end of World War II. William Shatner of *Star Trek* fame strolled by every day, but we had no idea he would become famous. With his good left hand, my father pointed to the ground coffee resting in the battered chrome bowl on top of the old Silex coffeemaker. I could see the sparse sprinkling of tiny white salt crystals speckling the dark brown surface. "Not more than a pinch, just like that."

I was too young to drink coffee, even though I loved the friendly smell of it. Besides, everything my dad made was great, so I presumed the coffee was as well. It's strange that so many decades later, I can still picture that bowl of fresh coffee grounds sitting on the old Silex.

Whenever I was around, my father would drink his coffee in a glass. It was a tiny ritual between us, because he normally had coffee in a cup like everyone else. But when I was there, he poured himself a glass of coffee, always with a spoon in it so the glass wouldn't crack from the sudden heat. He added a teaspoon of sugar and gave it a slow stir. Then, my favorite part—he slowly drizzled a thin stream of Carnation milk from the tiny can into the glass so I could see the slowly swirling patterns evolve and the color magically change from black to dark chocolate to a rich lava caramel. When it started to get homogenous, he gave it all a last stir, all the while getting great satisfaction out of my untiring amazement at the kaleidoscope of patterns that came out of a simple glass of coffee. Of course, that's not all I remember from that perfect summer working with my dad. It was also the first time I learned about proportional diplomacy— that particular talent of treating people exactly the way they should be treated.

My father was extremely popular with the clientele and always trading a joke or two with them. Almost all the factory workers were immigrants who toiled away doing the piecework that ended up in all the fashionable department stores around America. I remember taking my Little Flyer wagon filled with sandwiches, coffeepots, sugar, and Carnation condensed milk up the rattling elevator, getting off at every floor, and dragging it around while everyone filled up a cup, each one looking almost as if he had just been dragged out of a steaming shower. Despite their slave wages and unspeakable working conditions, they could always be depended on for a good laugh and were as honest as Abe Lincoln. When they got paid on Friday they all filed down to the stand to pay my father for their weeks takings. No one cheated.

Dad was everyone's hero, not because he had come to the country thirty years before they did, or because he gave them credit for a full week, but because he ran a small business and raised a family with only one hand. He had lost his right one in a munitions mishap years earlier. I remember asking him about the rounded salami-shaped stump at the end of his right forearm. "You know son, it's funny, I can still feel all my fingers," he would say looking down on it, without the least sound of sadness.

Besides the sweatshop workers, there were several wealthy shmata-business magnates in the building and by and large, they too had a great deal of respect for my father and were always asking him for an opinion on one thing or another. "Arthur, we just got in a shipment of fifty black suits from Hong Kong, but somebody messed up with the patterns. The backs aren't stitched properly.

They're a disaster and I already paid for them. What should I do?" My father would think for a minute. "Why don't you go see Collins Brothers, you know, the big undertakers on Park Avenue. They're always buying black suits and when they put some poor guy into a black suit in the box, believe me, nobody's going turn him over to check if the back is stitched properly." "Arthur, that's terrific! Gimme a coffee and let me buy you one too!"

My next run-in with coffee didn't occur until I was in college going through my beatnik phase. Bearded and smelling from every reagent chemical that the biochemistry lab had on its meager shelves, I'd sit up all hours of the night in my tattered lab coat in the Pam Pam Coffeehouse behind Sir George Williams University. The Hungarian owners boasted a variety of fifty-two different types of coffee from around the world and we would jokingly ask for "Instant Maxwell House." Without doubt, the owners sorely missed beautiful Budapest, and our thoughtless humor only heightened their sense of loss.

During graduate school my wife and I got married, and with all the money we had saved we managed to take a week's honeymoon at the beautiful Saxony Hotel in Miami Beach. It was the best summertime deal going for impoverished students, and I recall having the beautiful Oceanside penthouse suite with three fantastic meals a day for the two of us at a grand total cost of thirty-two dollars per day, state and local taxes included.

The first time we went down for breakfast we caught that drift of aroma in the elevator. What was that fantastic smell? It hit us face on as we entered the hotel's breakfast restaurant. That superb rich aroma of great American coffee! It almost smelled like the beans were being roasted in the restaurant. The coffee was unlike any we had before, and it was served in a bottomless cup. We kept eating just so that we could get more coffee. Unfortunately, that last vestige of great American coffee, like our honeymoon, became history and we were soon back to the same old grind.

It was never my intention to go into the food industry, but after leaving graduate school that's exactly what I did. I ended up directing research for a number of multinational corporations. In one of them, among the products we manufactured was roasted coffee, and that is where I first met my good friend Albert Dangoor. Albert and his family had emigrated from Iraq via London to Montréal. While in London, Albert learned the trade of a tea and coffee taster. I remember spending hours with him as he patiently taught me some of the finer points of tasting. We made very good coffee during that time but could never reproduce that particular flavor from the Saxony Hotel.

Oddly enough the next time my wife and I tasted great American coffee was when we were on a business trip to Japan. There, in the tiny posh President Hotel in Tokyo's Aoyama district, that elusive aroma from the past hit us. Somehow, the Japanese had managed to ferret out the secret that gave the best American coffee its extraordinary character and then they duplicated it. It was just like being back in the Saxony Hotel, except that the coffee was served in tiny white, wafer-thin porcelain cups that were anything but bottomless. In fact, we were charged seven bucks for every refill. We sipped it very, very slowly. As with our honeymoon in Miami, we left Tokyo and went back to humdrum boring coffee, some better, some worse.

After serving as president of a multinational milling company for a few years, I received a call from a friend in government that there might be a position open with the United Nations Food and Agriculture Organization in Rome, Italy. Having gone about as far as I wanted in the food industry, I discussed it with our expanded family and we all concluded it would be a great experience, so I applied for the job. After being called to Rome for an interview, I took advantage of the endless variety of cappuccinos, espressos, lungo macchiatos, and café corretos. Needless to say, I decided I had to stay just for the coffee, so in retrospect it's a good thing I got the job.

On one occasion, one of my American colleagues told me he was absolutely intent on frustrating our favorite barman. Italian barmen are known to be unflappable. If you ordered a sandwich and asked what the red stuff was, the barman wouldn't even look up from wiping off the counter and reply with complete authority, "Mayonnaise!" But my friend was determined to catch him off guard and worked on a script for three days. When he went up to the barman he blurted out, "*Mezzo, mezzo cappuccino e tè, forti, ma non troppo forti, con un po'di pesca e yogurt!*" (Half cappuccino and half tea, strong, but not too strong, with a bit of peach and yogurt!)

The barman looked him square in the eye and said in perfectly condescending English, "Finally, an American who knows what he wants!"

Coffee can do that for you.

Acknowledgments

I would like to thank Linda Regan of Prometheus Books for suggesting this book and for the endless work she put in editing it. I would also like to thank Ed Knappman of New England Publishing Associates, who, as always, provided helpful guidance and insight throughout its preparation. I would also like to express my sincere appreciation to Matt Brown and the staff of Mayorga Coffee Roasters in Rockville, Maryland, who were always open to my visits and allowed me free access to photograph their operations. Finally, I would like to thank my wife, Miriam, for her patience, understanding, and support throughout the course of writing this work.

Prologue

The clock must be off again. Feet feel like furniture dragging across a shag rug. What's with my back? It's so stiff. I don't even think a hot shower will help. What day is today? Whatever it is, I know something's wrong, I can feel it.

My eyes still feel swollen and the shower was useless. I'm still stiff all over. Even the skin on my face feels like Saran wrap stretched across a bowl. And what's with the shoes? They fit perfectly yesterday. Where's that dumb shoehorn? Forget the news. I know something's wrong.

I'd better start looking for a new machine, this thing is taking longer and longer. Filters, water, all set. I guess I'll have to get coffee this weekend. H'mmm, nice smell. Let's get the paper and see what it's like outside.

More and more ads. They have to cut down a small forest for one of these papers. Boy, that smell is always so beautiful. They should bottle it and sell it as a bedroom odorizer.

Finally! Which cup? What a stupid question. The big one, of course. I ought to get a new one but this one is so comfy. And it feels so good in my hands.

Cheers to another day. Ohhhh, that's good. That first intoxicating sip. The eyes are starting to see. What in the headlines? Let me see. M'mmm, that's good. Let's see, "Terrorists May Have Nuclear Weapons," "China and US on Brink of All-Out Trade War," "Economy Headed Down the Drain."

Man, this is good java! "Giant Greenland Fissure Due to Global Warming," "Medicare Declares Chapter Eleven." One last sip. Delicious.

That's better. Looks like it's gonna be a great day!

Why does coffee make the world seem right? And what is it about coffee that gives us so much satisfaction? Regardless of culture, whether you choose a small latte, an almond-flavored vente, a tin cup of cowboy joe, or a thimble of espresso ristretto, coffee just seems to make us feel better. It picks us up and relaxes us at the same time. You want to have a long sip and a soothing sigh? Go ahead, open your nostrils and breathe in deeply, you can open your eyes later. You want to get keyed up for the interview and remember all the answers you rehearsed? A quick shot of it will do. You want to revise the corporate strategic plan, work out the latest equations on relativistic string theory, or envision a bold move? Coffee will sharpen your mind, help you focus your thoughts, and give you the boost to drill down to the key issues. You can stuff the physicist's pipe, the philosopher's worry stones, and the poet's chewed pencils into the dustbin of history's bogus artifacts; it's java that has inspired many of our great intellectual breakthroughs. Coffee doesn't only wet the lips, it also whets the intellect.

Coffee also seems to encourage interactions between humans. How often have we heard, "Let's grab a cup of coffee and discuss it." It just works.

Because of its caffeine, coffee is often referred to as one of our very few legal drugs. Yet, the alkaloid it contains is found in a wide variety of soda pops, often at a higher dose, but is seldom considered the same. You are unlikely to hear, "You look upset, poor dear. Come, let's sit down and have a can of caffeinated energy drink."

There's no doubt that certain caffeine-containing drinks will keep you awake, which is handy when you're trucking from Memphis to Albuquerque through the night, or writing a couple of hundred lines of code to finish a program before the deadline. Both require routine thinking and practiced reflexes—not the creative blockbusting that coffee is capable of fueling. So does that make coffee a drug?

Drugs are considered to be chemical substances,

such as various alkaloids, that affect the central nervous system, causing changes in behavior and even addiction. But caffeine is far from the only alkaloid we routinely consume. Tea and cocoa both have the closely related alkaloids theophylline and theobromine, which have strong pharmacological properties similar to caffeine. Black pepper contains piperine, chavicine, and piperidine; potatoes have solanine; tomatoes feature tomatine; and yams boast dioscorine. Although these alkaloids can exert strong effects upon our metabolism and nervous systems, we hardly consider these products as drugs.

But because of caffeine, coffee is considered a legal drug, in fact, the most popular drug on the planet. But what kind of drug is it?

Is it a stimulant?

A stimulant is an agent, especially a chemical agent such as caffeine, that temporarily arouses or accelerates physiological or organic activity.

The answer is yes.

Is it a relaxant?

A relaxant is something, such as a drug or therapeutic treatment, that relaxes or relieves muscular or nervous tension.

Here again, the answer is yes.

Both a stimulant and a relaxant? Then it's not just caffeine that is affecting us. Based upon our experience with coffee, this makes sense. Coffee has always been a social lubricant, but unlike alcohol, the caffeinated interaction is productive. Socializing with coffee drinkers usually involves animated intellectual banter. It matters not whether the interaction is academic, political, commercial, or plain local gossip, coffee relaxes people enough to feel comfortable talking with one another while keeping thoughts clear and focused.

When consumed in reasonable amounts, coffee generally causes no harm, and the average person's tolerance for it is considerable. It has provided great enjoyment to billions of people over the centuries. Coffee has encouraged countless positive interactions that very likely led to great discoveries and inventions, immeasurably enriching our lives. Moreover, few would doubt that coffee's ability to keep people alert has saved an infinite number of lives.

We live in a world where change occurs at such a rapid rate that we take for granted even the latest developments right after seeing them. A little more than a generation ago, the only computers we had were housed in glass-enclosed rooms with special ventilation. We would look at them with awe. They were the property of companies or universities or government. Even an indepen dent consultant could not afford one. Today, primary school children in developing countries have computers more powerful than those in glass-enclosed rooms. Yet we take modern desktops and laptops for granted. The very idea of having a cell phone would be considered science fiction thirty years ago, but today, most are looking for the next generation iPhone or BlackBerry. These days, taking things for granted can be taken for granted.

Except for a great cup of coffee. Make a great cup of coffee and no one will take it for granted. Look at the Starbucks phenomenon. People who would otherwise never be bothered to utter a word in a foreign tongue are calling out, "I'll have a caramel latte," or "Please give me a cappuccino grande, doppio." Starbucks has done more for the Italian language than Donatella Versace.

America and the rest of the world are enjoying a renaissance in coffee. A beverage that lay dormant for decades has caught fire—everywhere. Whether it be a latte with a double shot, a cappuccino, an espresso macchiato, or a plain cup of black java, coffee is one of the world's most sought-after beverages. In North America and Europe, the volume of coffee consumption amounts to about a third of that of tap water![1] Not only has coffee remained popular in countries that have traditionally consumed it, but it has taken on phenomenal growth in developing economies, where little was previously consumed.

Remember the expression "I wouldn't do that for all the tea in China"? It was a reflection of the massive amount of tea grown and consumed in China. Times have changed. The rise in the number of working women and urban professionals in China resulted in total volume sales of coffee that grew by 90 percent in the five years between 1998 and 2003. Coffee sales continue to skyrocket in that country, fueling the drive behind part of its economic explosion. You can now find coffee everywhere in China. The same can be said for India, another traditional stronghold of tea drinking. Coffee drinking is starting to experience significant growth in consumption as the Indian economy moves into high gear. In fact, the winner of the 2002 World Barista Championship, a competition based on the art of espresso making, was Vikram Kurana of India.

What is it about coffee that makes it so popular across so many differing cultures? Where did it originally come from? Why is it a beverage that we can't seem to live without? Can it be just the caffeine or is there something else that makes it so alluring to us? The questions we have about coffee are legion.

Although there are many who believe that coffee originated in South America, that is a myth. Coffee's history can be traced back to ninth-century Africa, specifically the highlands of Ethiopia. From there it spread to Yemen, Egypt, Turkey, and the rest of the Middle East. Its popularity in the Muslim world was accelerated because coffee provided a simulating alternative to alcohol, which was prohibited.

From the Muslim world, coffee spread to Europe and eventually to America, where it had a difficult start because the hardworking colonists found it to be a rather poor substitute for the tea and alcohol they were accustomed to. This changed during the Revolutionary War, partly due to the criticisms of insobriety and particularly because of the reduced availability of tea from Britain. America's taste for coffee grew during the early nineteenth century. The demand was raised to new heights during the Civil War when soldiers in the field found it a comforting as well as warming drink that also kept them alert when standing guard. Advancements in brewing technology made coffee more palatable and firmly fixed coffee as a beverage of choice in the United States. Today, nothing exemplifies the act of getting out of bed then happily preparing for the day as does a cup of steaming hot coffee.

How has the habit of drinking coffee evolved to fit the social and economic needs of different times and places? In the intellectual capitals of the world, coffeehouses became the venues where the great minds flocked to discuss the latest developments in the arts, sciences, and social philosophies. Coffee was the magnet that drew people together for a spirited exchange of information and ideas. In office and factory settings, coffee was the beverage that gave weary employees that extra boost of energy to get them through the morning's or afternoon's work, and it still does. Coffee has evolved into a necessity of our modern, dynamic lifestyle.

While coffeehouses and bars retained their popularity in Europe, they began to decline in popularity in

North America during the second half of the twentieth century—until its last two decades. Using the Italian coffee bar as a model, the new coffee movement in America quickly introduced the terms cappuccino, latte, and espresso to the public. While Italian bars offer a café correto (coffee with a shot of whiskey), liquor laws required their American counterparts to provide different flavored alternatives instead.

The renaissance of coffee in America is evident in people walking everywhere with their large cups of coffee. People stride into meetings, do their window shopping, and get on airplanes, all holding that familiar cup of coffee.

Coffee is an extraordinary beverage that agreeably wakes us up in the morning, keeps us going throughout the day, and supplies us the energy to stay alert for late-night work or study sessions. It is the quintessential American brew that perfectly matches our on-the-go, nonstop work ethic. Whether we drink it out of habit, to bask in its exquisite flavor and aroma, or simply to get us through the day, coffee is surely one of nature's noblest creations and our most beloved beverage.

PART 1

Origins and History

1

The Agricultural Origins of Coffee

Foods that many of us eat, such as hot peppers, are so ubiquitous in our diets that there is a natural tendency to believe they originated in many different parts of the world independently. The blazing hot foods of Southern India, Sichuan China, Thailand, Indonesia, and Vietnam are typical examples. Because of this, most people believe that Asia was the origin of the various hot capsicum peppers responsible for the fiery flavor of foods from that region. Not so.

Up until about four hundred years ago, the "hottest" spice in Asia was the black peppercorn, a fairly mild condiment compared to the incandescent capsicums so common in today's Asian cuisine. Hot capsicum peppers all originated in Central and South America and the Caribbean. After the region was discovered by Christopher Columbus, the hot capsicum peppers were thought to be a great alternative to black pepper and quickly entered the intercontinental trade.

It was the Portuguese who introduced hot pepper into India and Asia and, consequently, their cuisine changed forever. So it was that hot peppers, corn, tobacco, potatoes, tomatoes, chocolate, and strawberries—all crops originating in the New World and discovered by Columbus—found new and permanent homes in different regions, countries, and cultures around the world.

Not long ago, I carried out a small, fairly unscientific survey among friends and neighbors to determine where they thought coffee may have originated from. About 75 percent thought that South America (Brazil or Colombia) was the region of origin, while 15 percent believed that it was Indonesia (specifically the island of Java). A grand total of 10 percent of the group mentioned Africa (referring to Kenya).

Most people are very surprised to learn that coffee originated in the Ethiopian Highlands, a large and rugged mass of mountains that occupies the center of the country. The highlands are distinguished from the rest of Africa by the extent of high ground they cover—approximately 203,000 miles^2—the size of Colorado and Wyoming combined. The geographic and cultural heartland of this region is an enormous plateau, averaging around 7,000 feet high and divided into two halves by the Great Rift Valley—that huge geographic trough, approximately 3,700 miles in length, that runs from northern Syria down to central Mozambique in East Africa.

A collection of unique plants, which produce best at altitudes between six thousand and seven thousand feet, originated and were domesticated in the Ethiopian Highlands, including khat (a stimulant seed), ensete (a bananalike food), noog (an oilseed), finger millet, and tef (a sorghumlike grain), in addition to coffee.[1] The exact date and location for the domestication of all these plants has been lost to history. However, on the basis of historical, geographic, and botanical studies, many researchers place the date somewhere between three thousand and six thousand years ago. The Ethiopian Highlands can be seen on the following map. There still remains some controversy regarding the first use of coffee and its earliest migration to other countries. However, most scientists agree that the cool volcanic Ethiopian Highlands are the original birthplace of our daily java.

The coffee plant is a striking example of migration and translocation of a valued commodity. We will soon learn of its fascinating travels to all corners of the world, but before that voyage begins, let's take a look at the story of its initial discovery. The discovery of coffee, in common with the discovery of many foods and beverages—particularly those with psychological effects—is steeped in different legends that have persisted throughout the centuries. Plants have been in our midst often for significant periods of time before their value

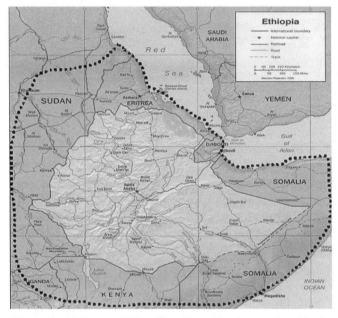

Shaded relief map of Ethiopia. (From the Perry-Castañeda Library Map Collection, University of Texas, Austin, a work of the Central Intelligence Agency.)

was recognized, and often these discoveries came about almost by accident.

Most of us remember the story of Sir Walter Raleigh and his discovery of potatoes by burning his crop of newly imported plants, which he thought to be useless.

Upon digging up the ground for replanting, his workers ended up discovering Europe's first baked spuds—pure serendipity and the foundation of one of our dietary staples. Botanical historians believe that the Olmecs of southern Mexico first discovered that the cocoa fruit was edible by watching rodents eat it with relish. They soon realized the tree produced a pod with a great number of different and exotic flavors that made a very tasty and stimulating drink.

It is most likely that coffee was first consumed as a food. The nomadic Galla tribe of the Ethiopian Highlands was the first group of people to recognize that consuming coffee beans had a sustaining effect. They gathered up coffee beans from local trees, ground them up, and mixed the resulting powder with animal fat to form small balls that they could carry around as a nutritious snack. However, it is not balls of ground raw coffee beans that for centuries have been one of the world's most adored consumables. That required an additional fortunate discovery. The story behind the discovery of coffee as the time-honored beverage we drink today is the stuff of fairy tales and legends, as it should be. The tale behind the discovery of coffee is fascinating and complex, and says much about the unique character of the beverage and the culture from which it emerged.

THE LEGEND OF KHALDI
AND HIS DANCING GOATS

Despite the volcanic origin of the Ethiopian Highlands, the winds and heavy exploitation by the local population over millennia made the land around Jimma, the capital of the Kaffa Province, sparse and of limited use to farmers. Scrub and dwarf bushes dotted the scant landscape. This sort of isolation was ideal for the religious monasteries established by the newly arrived religion of Islam. The inexorable flood of Islam into this formerly Christian kingdom had not taken long. According to Islamic tradition, some members of Muhammad's family and some of his early converts had taken refuge in Axum in 615 CE, during the troubled years preceding the Prophet's rise to power, and as a result, Axum was exempted from the holy war. Muhammad felt that Ethiopia was "a land of righteousness where no one was wronged."[2] It was not long before monasteries were built there to serve those who were righteous.

Barren as the land was, it ideally suited the habits of goats. Goats love to eat scrub, thistles, and blackberries, all of which are of high nutritional value and are not sought after by competitive grazers. Goats also eat weeds, which were plentiful in the region. In fact, goats will try to eat just about anything, a characteristic that eventually resulted in a great benefit for all of us.

Goats were ideally suited to the needs of the

monastery. Once fed upon the sparse vegetation, they provided the monastery with milk, which was converted into cheese, goat hair, which was woven into clothes and carpets, and leather and flexible skins used to make the vellum upon which the Koran was originally written. In return, the monastery provided the goats with herdsmen to guide them to food as well as to protect them from the wild beasts such as wolves and leopards that sought them out as food—a mutually beneficial relationship.

It happened one day that a young goat herder named Khaldi was tending to a flock that belonged to the nearby monastery. After taking his customary afternoon nap in the shade of some bushes, he set out to look for them in order to gather them in for the night. Searching far and wide, he was unable to find them. Knowing well he was certain to be thrashed if he returned with any of them missing, he continued to search frantically for them well into the night. They could have gone only higher up the plateau or else he would have been awakened by them while he dozed. With the help of the bright light of the full moon, he anxiously followed their trail. If wolves or leopards were about, now would be the time they would attack. His sweaty hand gripped his staff tightly as he pressed forward and upward.

Just as he was getting ready to trace his way empty-handed back down the slopes, he heard excited bleating up ahead, beyond some strange-looking, very thick bushes. He pressed forward and was greeted with the most bizarre sight that a young goat herder had ever seen, under the light of the bright Ethiopian moon.

All the goats, young and old, smooth skinned and shaggy, male and female, were gaily gamboling around butting heads and pronking about like young gazelles. Looking very much like their legs were made of springs, they all appeared to have the ceaseless energy of adolescents. The sight so amazed Khaldi that he totally forgot about the dangers associated with the night. Not seeing any apparent reason for their erratic behavior, he examined the leaves and berries on the bushes they were munching on and broke off a few to put in his pouch.

After watching them for a while, his concern for predators returned and he decided it was time to take his charges back down to the monastery. With great difficulty, he rounded them up and, tying a rope around the horns of his trained Judas goat, slowly led them back down the mountain.

When he got back down to the monastery, there was a reception waiting for him. A group of workers, monks, and the imam himself were getting ready to search for Khaldi since he had not returned when he should have. With some joy and considerable consternation they all cheered when he came into sight with his herd of goats. "Imam, Imam, forgive me, I have returned. And I have the strangest story for you. My goats—I saw them dancing like demons by the light of the moon!"

Probably as a result of their tedious and boring occupation, goat herders were known to have a tendency toward exaggeration and were more often than not considered to be inveterate liars. While everyone stood around and laughed, the imam glanced at the goats and saw that they were indeed in an agitated mood. "Khaldi, put your goats in the stone corral and go to bed. We'll have plenty of time to speak about your dancing goats tomorrow."

The next morning at breakfast, Khaldi's strange story did not change. He showed the head of the monastery the berries and leaves that he had picked and placed in his pocket. Amused, the imam asked Khaldi to show him where he had seen the goats dancing. So it was that Khaldi, the imam, his chief assistant, and a herd of goats went back up the mountain, where the herd had been happily feeding the day before.

Khaldi had no trouble finding the spot where the goats had been dancing under the bright moon the previous evening. The imam was surprised to see the large, luscious green bushes whose leaves resembled those of the laurel bush, except that they were quite a bit thicker and heavily ribbed. He noticed the delicate white flowers and little red berries on the tall bush. "Tell me Khaldi, is this what our goats have been feeding on?" the imam asked. Khaldi nodded in agreement. The imam immediately placed a handful of the berries into his mouth and began to chew them. He found them to have a thin, slightly sweet outside pulp and each contained a hard, light green pit that was actually two halves stuck together. He slowly began chewing them. They were hard and somewhat bitter, but other than that, they didn't seem to have any particular character. After another few minutes, he indicated that they had seen everything there was to see and should all head back to monastery for lunch. He privately scoffed to himself about Khaldi's silly little tale. Boys will be boys.

Later that afternoon, the imam noticed that he didn't suffer from the fatigue he normally experienced during afternoon prayers. He wasn't certain why but he immediately thought about Khaldi's dancing goats and went to see his assistant, who had taken the trouble to collect a bagful of the berries. The assistant was not in his room, but the imam was intrigued by a beautiful aroma he caught wafting in from the monastery's courtyard. There he saw his assistant quietly burning up the seeds he had collected. In panic, the imam ran over to him and cried, "What are you doing? Stop burning them!"

Caught totally by surprise, the assistant managed to pull most of the beans out of the fire. "Imam, I'm sorry, I did not know you wanted to keep them, so I put them in the fire. See what a beautiful smell they have! Perhaps we can burn them as incense!"

"No, no, no," the imam insisted. "I have a better idea." He had dabbled in alchemy in his younger days and thought the roasted beans might make an interesting and stimulating beverage. He bent down and cleaned off the burnt beans. He then took them to the monastery and pounded them in a brass mortar. The imam then stirred and steeped the resulting powder in hot water. The water quickly turned black. After a short period, he poured off the liquid and, together with his assistant, drank the strong, black brew.

They had never tasted anything like it. The aroma was pungent and captivating and the taste seemed to overtake all their senses. The assistant found it rather bitter and added some honey to sweeten it. That evening both the imam and his assistant conducted the most vigorous evening and nighttime prayers the monastery had ever experienced. They quickly moved about and chided the other participants for their laziness. While the sleepy monks could barely keep their eyes open, the imam and his assistant seemed to have unlimited reserves of energy. All night they prayed, the imam confident that Khaldi's goats had delivered a genuine miracle to his hands. He had discovered a true gift from the Prophet—a gift that allowed them to serve him at night with vigor and a clear mind as they had never been able to before.

So wrote the Maronite monk Antonius Faustus Nairon (1635–1707), professor of theology at the Sorbonne in his 1671 treatise, *Discurso sobre a salvherrima bebida chamada cahve, ov café*.

Is the story true? It certainly has been repeated often enough. In fact, the story was repeated in Johann Hübner's famous German encyclopedia *Curieuses und reales Natur- Kunst- Berg- Gewerck- und Handlungs-Lexicon*, published in 1717, only a decade after Nairon's death. It is impossible to say with any certainty how valid the story is, but it is a lovely one that totally fits in with the locale and circumstances of coffee's origin. Coffee was first discovered growing in the Ethiopian Highlands and found to have a stimulating effect on the senses. It gave those who consumed it freedom from weariness and a great deal of clear-minded energy. When roasted and consumed as a beverage, it was delicious, flooding the senses with a heady aroma and a rich, satisfying body. It was truly a wonderful discovery—surely a gift from a deity.

Khaldi and his gamboling goats were merely the lead-in. The heart of the story was the ready recognition by the imam of the unique properties and value of coffee. Here was the product of a natural plant that had the ability to sharpen and focus the senses. Not only did it have an alluring aroma and a wonderful taste, but it had the ability to extend alertness far beyond one's normal ability. It did not dull the mind nor did it encourage one to do things one would not normally do, as the wine of the infidels did. Coffee also allowed one to spend more time embracing the words and work of the great Prophet.

THE WINE OF ISLAM

In the Koran, a verse in the surah titled "The Table" stipulates that "the food of those to whom the Book (the Old Testament) was given is lawful for you, and yours for them." The reference here is most probably to the food rules in Genesis 1:29 and Leviticus 11:3, 11:7, and 17:12–14. Edible animals in these verses of the Old Testament are those that have cloven hooves and chew their cud. Likewise, the Koran prohibits the consumption of swine. Where the Old Testament and the Koran differ is in the consumption of foods or beverages that alter one's consciousness—specifically wine.

The use of wine is first described in Genesis 9 of the Old Testament. Even though there is an unpleasant demonstration by Noah of the effects of drunkenness, the consumption of wine is not forbidden, under ordinary circumstances. On the contrary, its use is encouraged, especially on all festive circumstances. It is prohibited for priests and judges, and then, only when they are engaged in the performance of their official duties.

The Christian church even went a step further, equating the wine of the grape with the blood of Christ. Wine plays an essential part in all religious ceremonies and is excluded from recommendations related to abstinence and asceticism. The Judeo-Christian view of life holds no jaundiced eye toward Dionysus or Baccus, those party animals of Greco-Roman tradition.

Not so for the world of Islam. The Prophet warns against consuming anything with psychoactive effects, although the Koran does not contain references to any foods (such as mushrooms) other than wine that may have such effects. Caution in the consumption of wine is prescribed in several verses, and at least three verses warn strongly against wine and encourage total abstention: "Satan seeks to stir up enmity and hatred among you by means of wine and gambling, and to keep you from the remembrance of God and from your prayers."[3] The existence of these verses coupled with interpretations of the collections of tradition have led to a prohibition of all alcoholic beverages among most Islamic denominations.

Whereas wine dulls your brain and makes you sleepy and lethargic, coffee keeps you awake for much longer periods and hones your wits to a razor sharpness. What could be better suited for the faithful of Islam but a stimulant? It is the exact opposite to the infidel's sordid wine, which results in his corrupt and intemperate character. Finally Islam would have its own drink, but a drink that would sharpen the intellect and resolve of its consumer. No, coffee drinkers would not fall over one another in a drunken stupor; they would retain their senses and feel a focused intellectual energy unlike any previously experienced.

Thus began the amazing story of coffee. The plant found growing wild in the scrubby highlands of Ethiopia would eventually become one of the world's largest and most highly valued agricultural commodities. A tall, nondescript bush with slender white flowers and small red berries that would not ordinarily attract the attention of passersby ended up, through a fortunate series of events, providing pleasure, satisfaction, and heightened consciousness to billions of people around the world over the centuries. Through the simple act of roasting, grinding, and steeping, the dull green beans contained within the berries were transformed into a brew with a rich, intoxicating aroma and an intense taste that stimulated the senses, cleared the mind, and allowed people to be at their best long past their normal capacity.

Some believe the name coffee is derived from the Kaffa Province of Ethiopia. In a great deal of the literature, the original name given to coffee by the Ethiopians was *bunn* (just like the coffee-making machine). It is also likely that boiled raw coffee beans and leaves were at one time consumed as an insipid tea because the energy-giving compounds are very soluble in water and are readily extracted. But this concoction is not one that found favor throughout history because of its lack of flavor. It was roasted ground coffee that appealed to everyone and this was the product that made its way around the globe and eventually into your home, office, restaurant, and social hangout.

Young coffee beans. (Copyright Arteki, 2006.
Used under license from FeaturePics.com.)

WHAT IS THE BOTANICAL ORIGIN
OF COFFEE?

From a biological perspective, coffee belongs to the
botanical family Rubiaceae, which has over six thousand
species. Most are tropical trees and shrubs that grow in
the lower levels of the forests. Other common members
of the family include the gardenias and several plants
that produce valuable alkaloids such as quinine and

other useful substances, but the plant genus *Coffea* is easily the most important member of the family from an economic standpoint.

The genus *Coffea* was first described by Carolus Linnaeus in 1747. Linnaeus gave a vivid account describing how it induces insomnia, makes the hands tremble, and causes strokes to those who drink it. But he also maintained that coffee was good for ridding oneself of hangovers, migraines, and worms. However, in a 1761 work providing a botanical and medical history of the coffee tree and its fruits, he concluded that coffee destroys the

Coffee flowers. (Copyright Arteki, 2006. Used under license from FeaturePics.com.)

appetite, promotes flatulence, and was noxious to depressed, hypochondriacal, and hysterical people.[4]

While Linnaeus was able to describe easily the effects of drinking coffee, he had considerably greater difficulty in arriving at its botanical classification. Problems arose for the designation of certain varieties as true members of the *Coffea* genus because of the tremendous differences that were seen in the plants and seeds. All species of *Coffea* are treelike, but they can range from small scraggly shrubs to large bushy trees over thirty feet tall. Even the leaves can vary in color, from a yellowish to a very dark green.

The two most important species of coffee in terms of economics are *Coffea arabica* (arabica coffee) and *Coffea canephora* (robusta coffee, a term derived from its ability to thrive in the harsh environment of the West African rain forest). Two other species are grown on a much smaller scale, *Coffea liberica* (liberica coffee) and *Coffea dewevrei* (excelsa coffee). Arabica coffee accounts for about 70 percent of world production at present.

Coffea arabica, universally considered to be the highest-quality coffee variety, was the first species of coffee to be cultivated in Arabia, and has continued to be grown there for more than a millennium. The mild character of this coffee variety is considered to be superior to the other common commercial variety, *Coffea robusta*. This latter species also has its origins in Africa, but west

Pollinating coffee flowers. (Copyright Arteki, 2006.
Used under license from FeaturePics.com.)

of Ethiopia. It is grown mostly in Africa and Brazil, as well as Southeast Asia. The largest producer is Brazil, followed by Vietnam. Since *Coffea robusta* is easier to maintain and has higher yields than *Coffea arabica*, it is cheaper to produce. Because of this, it is often used as an inexpensive substitute for arabica in commercial coffee blends. Good quality robustas are used in most Italian espresso blends to provide a better *crema* (foam head) and to lower the ingredient cost, but the capabilities of the coffee roaster have to be considerable in order to maintain an excellent flavor and bring out the best taste for this variety. Within each variety, the quality and character of the coffee will depend upon the agro-climatic conditions and the care and practice exercised by the grower. Certain varieties of arabica are particularly well known, such as the Jamaican Blue Mountain and Hawaiian Kona coffees.

Coffee plants generally grow to between ten to twenty feet tall with dark glossy green leaves that are very characteristic in shape and have thick, netted veins on the backside. The coffee flowers are rather small and white with a delicate fragrance. The five white flower petals are characteristically tubular in shape. While the normal color of coffee flowers is white, they occasionally may have a greenish or pinkish tinge, depending upon the weather.

The green oval berries are 0.4–0.6 inches long, and they turn yellow first, then bright red, and on to purple upon maturity. The anatomy of a coffee berry (often referred to as a coffee cherry) is quite complex. It has a thick outer portion called the *pericarp* that is made up of the surface skin under which lies a gelatinous pulp. This pulp is made up of thin-walled cells capable of taking up

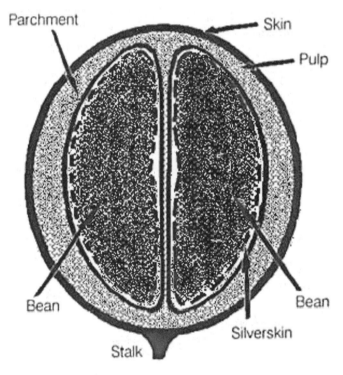

Cross section of a coffee berry. (© Morton Satin, 2008.)

large amounts of water. Directly beneath this is a thin parchment over a fine silver skin that covers the actual beans. Berries generally ripen within nine months. Each berry usually contains two seeds, but about 10 percent of the berries have only one seed and those are referred to as peaberries.

In the past, the coffee berry residue was discarded after the beans were removed, but now the pulp is being processed into liquids and powders that are marketed as health products. This is no surprise because the pulp is high in antioxidant content and is added to some coffee-based beverages, energy bars, and other foods. It is even used in cosmetics. The pulp extract apparently has the highest antioxidant potential of any food ingredient based on its Oxygen Radical Absorbance Capacity Score.[5] This score was developed by the US Department of Agriculture to measure the antioxidant capacity of natural substances. The pulp is therefore a more functional antioxidant than green tea, white tea, or grape seed extract.

THE PROCESSING OF COFFEE

Coffee trees usually begin to flower and grow fruit in three to four years after they've been planted, although a commercially practical harvest takes five years after the original planting. Once the flowers bloom, the green cherries emerge and mature within about eight months. In doing so, they change their color from green to deep red. When they reach this stage, they must be harvested. Although most countries have one major harvest a year, some fortunate countries such as Colombia will get two flowerings a year, allowing for a secondary harvest.

The ripe coffee cherries are usually handpicked, an exhausting and very poorly paid activity. Only cherries at the peak of their ripeness are harvested, with the workers rotating among the trees every week to ten days. This results in an extremely labor-intensive harvest used primarily for the more costly arabica beans. The coffee pickers generally receive payment per basketful of coffee cherries harvested. Since green cherries are frowned upon, pickers are penalized for including them.

In very large operations where the cultivated land is flat, such as Brazil, the picking process has been mechanized. Here, the entire crop is harvested at once. The mix of green and red berries or, in some cases, just green berries, are used to mass produce cheaper coffee beans, which are decidedly inferior in taste and aroma. The importance of the type of picking cannot be underestimated as it is the chief determinant in the final quality of the finished product.

Coffee beans are processed in two ways—"dry" and "wet." The dry process, sometimes called unwashed, or natural, processing, has been used for centuries. The harvested cherries are first sorted and cleaned to remove the

Raking dried coffee beans.
(Used under license from FeaturePics.com

unripe and spoiled cherries as well as dirt, twigs, and leaves. This can be done by winnowing, using a coarse sieve, or by flotation in water. The cherries are then spread outside for fifteen to twenty days, exposed to the sun in order to dry. They are then raked regularly to help them dry evenly. Once dried, the cherries are then dehulled by hand or by machine to remove the dried pulp and thin parchment.

With the wet process, the cherries are harvested and the pulp is removed within a few hours. This process requires special equipment and a good deal of water. The result is higher quality, more hygienic coffee beans that are better preserved. After the coffee beans are picked, they are sorted by water immersion. The spoiled or unripe cherries float to the surface while the good, mature fruit sink. The fruit is then squeezed by machine through a wet screen to remove the skin and some of the pulp. The remaining pulp is removed in a process that involves cycles of fermentation and rinsing, or a newer method of mechanical pulp removal called *aqua-pulping*.

Small amounts of fermentation don't hurt the beans, but the process has to be carefully monitored to ensure that the coffee won't acquire undesirable, off flavors. This method ends with the twenty-four to thirty-six-hour removal of the sticky, sugary layer of mucilage, the time involved being dependent upon the ambient temperature, the amount of pulp to be removed, and the rate of fermentation. The completion of the process is signaled by the feel of the parchment, which loses its slippery, slimy texture. When the fermentation is complete, the coffee is thoroughly washed and then sun-dried or mechanically dried to reduce the moisture down to 12.5 percent.[6]

The last stages of processing prior to bagging are hulling to remove the fine parchment, followed by cleaning, screening, sorting, and grading operations. High-speed electronic-eye sorting machines are often used to remove defective beans. Coffee beans are then graded on the basis of various criteria such as size, origin, method of harvest, and processing, and finally, how good they taste. Beans are usually exported in jute bags to roasting facilities, most often located overseas. Beans that don't qualify as "export" grade are usually used locally.

As an internationally traded commodity, coffee production (in excess of 13 billion pounds of coffee per year) ranks second in value only to oil.[7] Coffee cultivation takes place in about fifty tropical countries, where often it represents the main source of export earnings.

AGING COFFEE

From early on in its history, the movement of coffee from producer to consumer usually entailed a long and time-consuming sea voyage. As a result, green coffee beans were routinely more than a year old before they were roasted. The long journey exposed the coffee beans to different winds and changes in humidity, which had an impact on the flavor of the beans after roasting. The process of green bean aging remains controversial up to the present day. Many say that aging the coffee beans reduces acidity, while others feel that aging can result in off flavors. Since coffee is grown in tropical countries, musty warehouse conditions are not uncommon. As a consequence, great care must be taken during the aging process.

Several coffee producers sell coffee beans that have been aged for as long as three years or more. However, most experts believe that green coffee starts to lose its flavor after one year due to losses in the beans' essential oil content. Because coffee drinking is such a personalized taste, aging will be a factor in the overall appreciation for some people.

COFFEE ROASTING

Although much of coffee lore is devoted to the variety and geographic origin of specific coffee bean production, there is no doubt that a key to superb coffee lies in the roasting process. During the roasting, the green beans

Finished coffee beans. (© Morton Satin, 2008.)

puff up to nearly double their original size and are totally transformed in color, taste, and smell. Heating precipitates a chemical reaction known as hydrolysis, which fragments large molecules through the addition of hydrogen and hydroxyl ions, the elements of water. The starches are hydrolyzed into sugars while the proteins are denatured to alter the entire cellular structure of the bean. The process results in the release of coffee oil, or *caffeol*, the core of coffee's flavor from within the beans'

Getting beans ready to roast. (© Morton Satin, 2008.)

cells. Natural sugars are then caramelized, which adds to the color, flavor, and body.

Coffee roasters are typically large rotating horizontal perforated pans that have flat blades located a short height from the surface in order to tumble the coffee beans in a current of very hot air. Some roasters derive their heat from electricity or gas. Some older roasters continue to be wood fired. Regardless of whether they process single batches or operate in a continuous mode, or whether they are direct or indirect fired, all roasters operate at temperatures that range from 350 to 550°F. The beans are routinely roasted for about eight to thirty minutes.

Fresh out of the roaster. (© Morton Satin, 2008.)

Cooling roasted beans. (© Morton Satin, 2008.)

Coffee undergoes dramatic chemical changes during roasting. More than eight hundred compounds are formed with almost a third of them being aromatic in nature. The roasting process has two important phases, known as "cracks." During the initial phase of roasting, the green beans slowly dry, turn yellowish, and begin to smell a bit like popcorn. The second step, in which the beans double in size, occurs at around 400°F and is called the first crack because of the sound that is made. The beans turn a light brown color and lose about 5 percent of their weight. In the next stage, the temperature increases to approximately 430°F and their color goes from a light to a medium brown. At this temperature, the process of pyrolysis occurs, resulting in major changes to the chemical composition of the bean. This second step is followed by a second pyrolysis (called the second crack) occurring between 440 and 450°F. The color of the roasted beans is now medium-dark brown, and they take on an oily luster.

It is the roaster's art that makes the coffee so wonderful. There are certain points in the process that are very critical. Depending upon the growing, harvesting, processing, and distribution conditions, the character of every delivery of green beans may change, even if they are the same variety from the same region. The roaster will usually take a small sample from a new shipment of green beans and do a test roasting in a small laboratory in order to determine how to roast them. Too dark and the caramelized sugars will remove sweetness and add a harsh bitterness. Too light and there will be a lack of flavor and body. Sometimes the process is so critical that the heating is immediately followed by a short spray of cold water to instantaneously stop the second pyrolysis, or second crack, and prevent burning. There are many tricks to the trade that come only with experience and continual experimentation.

While it is clearly defined as a highly complex scientific process, coffee roasting still remains a true culinary art. Every shipment is different and requires a sensitivity to its specific needs for roasting. On top of that, the coffee producer must have an ability to blend various beans in order to arrive at a final product that will meet the needs of different consumers in terms of flavor, body, aroma, appearance, and price. It's not an easy task and it's not learned overnight. It can take years if not decades to really know how to romance the bean.

2

The Chemistry and Health Benefits of Coffee

offee—that beverage so dear to so many of us— is one of life's simple pleasures. However, when we examine it from a chemist's point of view, we find that coffee is the furthest thing from simple. Coffee's chemical composition is unbelievably complex and we have only started to uncover its secrets. Considerable gaps still remain in our understanding of coffee's scientific nature.

Coffee cherries, the fruit of the coffee plant, are generally picked by hand, sun-dried, then depulped to release the two raw coffee beans contained within each bean.

The chemical makeup of a cup of coffee will be dependent upon differences in the composition of the initial green beans, the changes that have taken place during its shipping and storage, the roasting process employed in that particular area, and the method for making the final cup—that is, the extraction process. Depending on the amount of water used to make the cup of coffee, the individual components will be diluted accordingly. Coffee variety and the manner in which it is consumed will vary with the social habits and culture of different countries. Because its consumption has spread to so many places around the world, great differences can be found in the taste and body of coffees.

The importance of the preparation method cannot be overstated because from the same roasted coffee totally different flavors and compositions will result. These will depend on the method used to extract the coffee, be it via espresso maker, filter machine, percolator, French press, vacuum coffeemaker, or even the Turkish method of boiling fine grounds. Minor differences in water temperature and the length of extraction time will create major differences in the final cup.

One thing we can all generally agree upon is that coffee must be roasted to be drinkable. Even though the green beans contain the psychoactive component caffeine, if they were ground without roasting and extracted with hot water, the resulting brew would have a disgustingly harsh, astringent-beany flavor that hardly anyone would ever drink voluntarily. Green coffee beans are even unpalatable when simply chewed.

The basic chemical composition of the two main types of raw coffee beans is shown in the following table:

TABLE 2.1. COMPOSITION OF RAW COFFEE ON A DRY BASIS[1]

Component	Arabica (%)	Robusta (%)
Polysaccharides	50.0–55.0	37.0–47.0
Lipids	12.0–18.0	9.0–13.0
Proteins	11.0–13.0	11.0–13.0
Oligosaccharides	6.8–8.0	5.0–7.0
Chlorogenic Acids	5.5–8.0	7.0–10.0
Minerals	3.0–4.2	4.0–4.5
Aliphatic Acids	1.5–2.0	1.5–2.0
Caffeine	0.9–1.2	1.6–2.4
Trigonelline	1.0–1.2	0.6–0.75

Of course, there will be variations in composition due to environmental factors such as soil, humidity, and altitude. As an example, a higher altitude results in cooler temperatures, which means slower growth and larger beans with more natural sugars. Because the sugars become metabolized into acids, higher altitudes result in greater acidity and fruitiness in the cup. Volcanic soils such as those found in Guatemala or Hawaii bring a distinct flavor to the coffee, as does the amount of humidity and rainfall.

HOW ROASTING CHANGES COFFEE'S COMPOSITION

Roasting is what makes coffee, coffee. It is roasting that has made coffee the valued international commodity that it is. The roasting process dramatically changes everything about it. Although a great deal of the process can be explained in terms of changes to physical and chemical composition, roasting changes the character of the bean so much as to make it almost unrecognizable from the original pale green seed from which it started. The most important changes to take place result from a chemical process called the Maillard reaction.

The Maillard reaction was first discovered by the French chemist Louis Camille Maillard in 1912. He was the first to characterize the reaction that occurs between carbohydrates (sugars) and proteins when they are heated together—a reaction responsible for most of the changes in color and flavor that take place when food is cooked. Technically, the Maillard reaction is classified as a nonenzymatic browning reaction because it occurs in the absence of enzymes. The carbonyl group of the sugar reacts with the amino group of the amino acid and forms a large variety of compounds responsible for aromas and flavors. Whether it is the intense flavor on the surface of roasted meat or the change in flavor when toast goes from a light tan to a golden brown to a burnt crust, it is chiefly the result of the Maillard reaction. However, nowhere is the Maillard reaction more important than in coffee because such a great number of volatile substances are produced in the roasting process. Collectively, they result in coffee's delightfully complex aroma and rich, dark color.

While the overall contents of caffeine and the lipid components change very little throughout the process, roasting dramatically modifies the quantities of the sugars and amino acids—the two components involved in the Maillard reaction. It is rather amazing that the chemical condensation of the sugars' carbonyl groups and the amino groups of the proteins' amino acids can produce so many volatile and pigmented compounds.

Coffee's aroma results from its volatile compounds that are perceived by our olfactory senses as flavor or odor. Our nose has thousands of sensory cells in the mucosa of the nasal cavity. Molecules of aroma pass through the nasal passages and dissolve in the mucus lining of the nasal cavity. They are then detected by sensory cells or olfactory receptors on the olfactory nerve endings.

The olfactory receptors can be simulated directly upon inhaling the molecules that rise up with the steam from your cup. When you drink coffee, the volatile substances reach the nasal cavity through the nasopharyngeal passage. Your nose picks up the aromas from the coffee and translates them into nerve impulses that are then sent to the olfactory bulb in the brain. The olfactory bulb, located in the front of the brain, communicates the smells to other parts of the brain. Dr. Linda Buck, winner of the 2004 Nobel Prize in Physiology and Medicine, has demonstrated the signal that the brain responds to is not the input from a single neuron but is from a group of neurons. Using brain imaging techniques researchers have found that different smells produce different patterns of activation in an area that processes smell deep inside the brain called the piriform cortex. To the piriform cortex, coffee aroma has its own distinctive pattern. The volatiles that make up an aroma result in a mixture of brain patterns that coalesce into a single sensation.

More than a thousand volatile compounds have thus far been identified in roasted coffee. Although only forty or so are chiefly responsible for the overriding aroma, many others contribute to the nuances. These compounds include beta-damascenone (which has a cooked applelike aroma), 2,3-butanedione (a buttery note), 2-furfurylthiol (a roasted, sulfury note), 2-isobutyl-3-methoxypyrazine (an earthlike note), guaiacol (a spicelike note), and 4-hydroxy-2,5-dimethyl-3(2H)-furanone (a caramel-like note).[2]

The following diagram is a gas chromatic analysis of the head space of fresh roasted coffee showing the many compounds (the individual spikes in the pattern, including the tiny ones) that contribute to its intoxicating aroma.[3]

TASTING COFFEE

While it is beyond our purpose here to turn the reader into a professional coffee taster, it is interesting to learn the process used in evaluating the aroma, flavor profile, and body of coffee. The process has the charming name of "cupping." Ideally, you would have samples of roasted beans from various parts of the world to "cup" side by side so that you could easily tell the difference between them.

There are always small idiosyncratic changes to the techniques employed in cupping. The taster that I worked closely with back in the 1970s always used small, thin white porcelain cups, very similar to those used for tea tasting. These days we normally see cupping carried out in small clear glasses so that one might see the color of the final product a little better.

The first thing carried out is sample preparation. This is done by placing 2 tbsp of freshly roasted and ground coffee in a 6 oz. cup. The idea is to use 5½ g of coffee (0.2 oz.) per 100 milliliters (3.4 oz.) of water. The grind should be between medium and fairly coarse, that is, halfway between a drip and a French press grind. When comparing coffees, you obviously have to use the same roast and grind size for all varieties or else the analysis would be meaningless. This gets a little tricky because some varieties cup better at different degrees of roasting. An easy way to compare the way they are all roasted is to put a spoon of each grind beside one another on a white surface then press them all down with a clear glass. This squishes them down adjacent to one another and immediately shows very subtle differences in the degree of roast between the various coffees.

While the water is boiling, it is a good time to smell the coffee grounds and record your impression of their fragrances.

Once the water is boiled, wait about ten seconds then add it to each cup. Quickly and carefully sniff each cup without disturbing the surface and record your first impression of the coffee's smell. After a minute has passed you can mix up the coffee with a spoon. Immediately bring your nose right on top of the cup and carefully record your observations of the aroma in as much detail as you can. Descriptions, such as "a smooth, mellow palate with clear hints of dark chocolate, blueberries, and a touch of ripe citrus peel at the finish" are used. They may sound a bit over the top, but it is important to try and express every sensation you perceive. Descriptions come considerably easier with experience.

Repeat the same process for all the cups.

The next task is a bit tougher. Once the coffee has cooled sufficiently to taste it, ladle some into a spoon and forcefully slurp it so that it is fully aspirated into the mouth. The idea is to get a bit of a vacuum on the fluid so that the volatile aromas come out. Unfortunately, it is one of the easiest ways in the world to choke yourself! Eventually with enough practice, you will get to do this without risking your life. After you taste each cup, spit out the coffee into a waste receptacle, record your observations, and move on to the next cup. Try to compare several different cups. Taste the cups once more after they have cooled a bit because they should have different characteristics at different temperatures. (I happen to like my coffee a bit cooler because the taste seems to linger longer.)

Most people incorrectly believe that acidity is a negative characteristic of coffee. In fact, acidity is a very desirable characteristic that describes the liveliness or boldness of coffee. Coffee with more acidity has an intense, pleasant aftertaste. A coffee that has less acidity is generally considered smoother. Coffees with very little acidity are often described as flat.

The body of a coffee refers to the sensation it provides when it settles on the tongue and palate. Coffee with more body has a thicker, more viscous quality that creates a sensation of smooth richness in the mouth. Body is the result of the coffee oils that are extracted during brewing. Methods such as espresso extract more oils and provide a more full bodied cup. The ubiquitous filter drip machine ends up with less body because the paper filter absorbs more of the coffee oils.

The ability to detect more and more nuances and tones develops with time. What is most important is to try and record your observations consistently. In a nutshell, that is cupping, but professional tasters will assure you that it can take a lifetime to perfect, and I believe them.

A taster's work is not in vain because millions of people all around the world enjoy nothing more than to start the day with a delicious, steaming cup of coffee. That wonderful aroma, exhilarating taste, eye-opening lift, and common experience of looking forward to a day's start with coffee have all become a vital part of our modern culture.

But coffee is far more than just a pleasing, invigorating beverage. In addition to its delightful sensory characteristics, there is significant authoritative information available demonstrating that drinking coffee has many benefits for our health and well-being.

COFFEE AND HEALTH

Appearance of the Patient

When a patient is given an average dose of caffeine, or when a strong cup of coffee is taken, the following effects are noticed:

The patient is wide awake, brighter, and is able to think more quickly and better, and to reason better. In fact, all mental work can be done better and with less fatigue. The patient is more active and responds more easily, more rapidly and better, to all influences around him. The pulse is quicker and may be stronger, and the breathing is deeper and more frequent. The patient also urinates more frequently and the quantity of urine is increased.

Caffeine is an ideal stimulant, because it increases the activity of almost every organ of the body.[4]

Not all medical descriptions of coffee and caffeine have been so flattering. Because coffee has always had the ability to mentally stimulate, it has always also been under suspicion from the point of view of health. Although coffee has many components, suspicion has always fallen on its main alkaloid, caffeine. Historically, caffeine has been one of the most heavily studied ingredients in our entire food supply. Despite centuries of safely consuming coffee, tea, and other beverages, misperceptions and concerns about caffeine's potential negative health effects continue to exist.[5]

Caffeine naturally occurs in the leaves, seeds, and fruits of more than sixty plant species around the world. The ones we are most commonly exposed to are coffee, tea, cocoa, and kola nuts.

Caffeine was first extracted and purified from coffee beans in 1819 by Friedlieb Ferdinand Runge, one of the nineteenth century's greatest chemists. Strangely, he made the discovery as a result of an encounter with the famous poet Goethe, who asked him to find out what it was that gave coffee beans their particular effect.

Today, the average per capita consumption of caffeine by American consumers is approximately 120 mg per day, slightly more than you would find in an average cup of home-brewed filter coffee. Of course, children don't consume nearly as much caffeine as adults do, despite the fact that they are great drinkers of caffeine-containing carbonated beverages, such as colas. The average intake of children between the ages of six and nine is about 22 mg per day and drops down to 14 mg per day for children one to five years of age. Between the ages of one to nine years carbonated beverages are the primary source of caffeine, while coffee serves that purpose for those twenty-five years and above. The shift from soft drinks to coffee occurs over the ages of ten and twenty-five years.[6]

In addition to coffee, tea, and carbonated beverages, new caffeinated energy drinks are starting to make market inroads. These beverages provide the possibility of easily doubling or tripling our normal intake of caffeine. A regular cup of home-brewed filter coffee will generally provide between 65 and 120 mg of caffeine, while a 12 oz. soft drink will provide from 35 to 70 mg of caffeine. On the other hand, caffeinated energy drinks can easily provide 100 to 300 mg or more of caffeine per serving. Tea drinkers can expect to find somewhere between 20 and 60 mg in a cup of their favorite brew, and a 1 oz. milk chocolate bar will have about 6 mg of caffeine.

The most typical effect of caffeine is the ability to improve alertness and mental concentration. Not only does it make consumers mentally sharper, but it also makes them feel better about the world. It improves their energy and, as most of us have witnessed, it improves their efficiency. But these effects are not necessarily transitory. Recent studies have shown that women who drink three or more cups of coffee per day have a slower rate of decline in mental abilities as they age.[7]

Some people believe that the rush coffee and caffeine provides often triggers feelings of anxiety. However, with the exception of extremely high consumptions (1,000–2,000 mg of caffeine per day), this has never been consistently demonstrated. And even with very high consumption rates, feelings of anxiety are rarely seen with most consumers.

As many of us have experienced, drinking coffee late in the evening can interfere with sleep. A great many people, however, are totally insensitive to caffeine and can drink it with impunity at all hours of the night and immediately enter into a comfortable sleep. We all differ greatly in our sleep sensitivity to caffeine. This sensitivity is no longer apparent after eight hours, so most people can comfortably drink coffee in the afternoon without any fear of disturbing their sleep routines. On the other hand, this characteristic of coffee is used to great advantage in keeping sleepy people alert, which is the reason why it is the most ubiquitous beverage consumed by long-distance truck drivers.

Caffeine is pharmacologically active as a mild stimulant. It also has the interesting ability to aid the body in the rapid assimilation of other drugs, which is why caffeine is often added to pain killers—to make them work faster. Once ingested, caffeine is rapidly absorbed and can readily pass through the blood-brain barrier. Within the body it is pretty rapidly metabolized with a half-life of about five hours. Some people believe that if coffee is withheld, they will experience withdrawal symptoms, such as headaches. Most of these concerns are based upon anecdotal evidence, because there is no convincing medical evidence that this effect takes place across a broad range of consumers. For those people who feel they get withdrawal symptoms, these can be dramatically reduced if withdrawal takes place slowly. Again, so much depends upon individual sensitivity.

Because of its stimulating effect and the sense that many experience withdrawal symptoms, it has often been questioned whether caffeine is addictive. This question has been reviewed by the American Psychiatric Association, but their researchers have not found sufficient evidence to demonstrate any clinical form of caffeine dependence.[8]

A great deal of research has been carried out to see if there is any link between the consumption of coffee and cardiovascular disease. Research results indicate that no adverse cardiovascular health affects result from the moderate intake (400 mg caffeine per day or less) of coffee. Of course, this does not mean that consuming more than moderate amounts will result in adverse effects—it only means that these higher intakes have not been studied sufficiently as yet.

Although caffeine consumption can result in a spike in blood pressure, this is only transitory and blood pressure returns to normal after a short period of time. There is little evidence that regular consumption of coffee will result in a chronic hypertension condition. The American Heart Association has developed a policy stating that the relationship of caffeine to coronary heart disease is still under study, despite a lack of evidence linking the two. This is not the first time that the American Heart Association has come up with a policy based on opinion rather than scientific evidence.

Children consume far less caffeine than adults. Even today many parents believe that caffeine is not good for kids. That fear notwithstanding, research shows that children (with the exception of infants), including those considered to be hyperactive, have roughly the same sensitivity to caffeine as adults do—that is, very little. On the other hand, caffeine has been shown to have a very positive cognitive effect on children, particularly with attention tests. Health Canada has suggested daily caffeine intakes for children at twice the levels currently consumed.[9]

Research on a possible link between cancer and caffeine has most often been conducted on coffee. Because the coffee-roasting process produces so many pyrolysis products (although in very small amounts) that are *potentially* carcinogenic,[10] it is extremely difficult to separate out the specific effects of caffeine. The few references there are on cancer related to caffeine are in most cases negative, that is, caffeine has not been shown to be carcinogenic.

A recent comprehensive review concluded that caffeine is unlikely to be a human carcinogen at levels below five cups of coffee per day (or less than 500 mg caffeine per day).[11] Added evidence indicates that caffeine, in the form that it is present in coffee, does not cause bowel, breast, pancreatic, bladder, or ovarian cancer. On the contrary, some recent studies have demonstrated a reduced risk of colorectal cancer with coffee consumption.[12]

A great many people suffer from occasional heartburn after drinking coffee. Researchers involved in a large Australian survey reported that heartburn was aggravated by a number of factors, including overeating, smoking, alcohol, stress, pregnancy, and spicy, greasy, or rich foods in addition to coffee. Therefore caffeine *per se* is an unlikely causative factor. In fact, there is a greater incidence of heartburn related to very dark roast coffee, which generally has less caffeine than lighter roasts.[13]

For people who suffer from GERD (gastroesophageal reflux disease) some studies suggest that consuming decaffeinated coffee may reduce symptoms for certain individuals. Nonetheless, the most convincing guidance comes from a large metareview covering 2,039 studies from 1975 to 2004 that found the only thing that really helps people with GERD is sleeping with the head elevated. Removing caffeine from the diet did not improve GERD symptoms, leading the authors to conclude that "there is insufficient evidence to support the routine recommendation that patients with GERD avoid caffeinated beverages."[14]

There is considerable evidence that consumption of coffee prior to physical exercise can improve endurance. It is possible that caffeine lowers the threshold for exercise-induced betaendorphin release, resulting in a quicker "runner's high." In driving and industrial work simulations, caffeine in amounts greater than 220 mg has been found to significantly improve performance.[15] Consuming 350–500 mg of caffeine can significantly increase endurance during both brief intense as well as extended exercises.

Perhaps the issue of greatest concern is the impact of coffee on the health of women, particularly those who are of childbearing age. For a time, it was believed that the caffeine in coffee might be responsible for such problems as miscarriage, premature birth, delayed conception, and birth defects. However, a comprehensive review concluded that these problems were more likely due to confounding factors, such as smoking, that were not accounted for in the studies.[16] The only conclusive studies done on birth defects were carried out in rats intravenously injected with caffeine at levels that are virtually impossible to duplicate in a human diet.

Epidemiological studies indicate that consumption of caffeine at or below 300 mg per day (approximately 3 cups of coffee) did not reduce fertility in women. However, a study on the effects of combined alcohol and caffeine consumption did show a significant risk for fertility that was not observed when caffeine was consumed alone.[17]

One of the greatest concerns that pregnant women have regarding coffee is the threat of miscarriage as a result of studies that have shown significant associations between caffeine intake greater than 300 mg per day and the risk of miscarriage. Other studies have not observed this effect. The issue is further complicated by the fact that nausea due to pregnancy leads to coffee aversion by some women, thus having a self-regulating effect on overall consumption.[18]

Reviews of all the evidence repeat the concerns that confounding artifacts, such as smoking or alcohol consumption, interfere with the analysis. The topic still remains controversial, but the overwhelming body of evidence indicates that maternal consumption of up to 300 mg per day of caffeine, or approximately three cups of coffee, is not likely to increase the risk of miscarriage. As a result, the Organization of Teratology Information Specialists states that consuming 300 mg per day of caffeine should not affect chances of miscarriage. However, the March of Dimes is somewhat more conservative in recommending that pregnant women limit caffeine consumption to less than 200 mg per day (two cups of coffee).[19]

The American Academy of Pediatrics Committee on Drugs recommends that nursing women limit their consumption of caffeine to three cups of coffee per day. The solubility of caffeine is such that it can easily permeate into breast milk, but nursing mothers can, according to the committee, safely consume limited quantities of coffee without passing on a significant amount of caffeine to the baby.[20]

Pregnant women are always concerned about the development of the fetus, and rightly so. When the impact of caffeine on fetal development was studied, however, no relationship could be found with caffeine intake. Smoking and high intakes of coffee together is another story. The overall conclusion is that coffee should be kept at moderate intake of three cups per day or fewer and smoking is forbidden.[21]

Most studies have indicated that normal coffee consumption is not related in any way to bone deterioration. However, during pregnancy and even later in life it is not a bad idea to add milk (even skim milk) to coffee as it will add to the total consumption of calcium.

BENEFITS OF
COFFEE CONSUMPTION

While there is a general tendency to focus on the possible negative impacts of coffee or caffeine consumption, we should note that there are a number of very significant positive effects, aside from keeping you awake longer and making you work more effectively.

Both caffeinated and decaffeinated coffees have been shown to reduce insulin sensitivity and may be beneficial to those with diabetes. Studies indicate that habitual coffee consumption improves glucose tolerance. This means that the body's ability to metabolize carbohydrates is increased, thus reducing the risk of diabetes. Large cross-country studies in the Netherlands, Finland, Sweden, and the United States have found that coffee consumption can reduce the risk of developing type 2 diabetes by as much as 55 percent for men and 79 percent for women. These are very significant results, particularly considering that insulin resistance, leading to type 2 diabetes, has started to reach epidemic proportions in the United States.[22]

The Health Professionals Follow-Up Study comprising 41,934 men and the Nurses' Health Study carried out with 84,276 women were designed to study the relationship between coffee consumption and type 2 diabetes. Results indicated that men who drank at least six cups of coffee per day had a 54 percent lower risk of developing type 2 diabetes than those who did not drink coffee at all. Women who drank six or more cups of coffee per day had a 29 percent lower risk than women who did not drink any. Strangely, tea consumption did not affect type 2 diabetes risks at all in either study. Several other studies came to similar conclusions strongly suggesting that coffee consumption can significantly lower the risk for type 2 diabetes.

A new study published in the *Annals of Internal Medicine* indicates that regular coffee drinking (up to six cups per day) is not associated with increased deaths in either men or women. On the contrary, researchers found that both caffeinated and decaffeinated coffee consumption is associated with a somewhat smaller rate of death from heart disease.[23]

"Coffee consumption was not associated with a higher risk of mortality in middle-aged men and women. The possibility of a modest benefit of coffee consumption on heart disease, cancer, and other causes of death needs to be further investigated," said Esther Lopez-Garcia, PhD, the study's lead author.

Women consuming two to three cups of caffeinated coffee per day had a 25 percent lower risk of death from heart disease during the follow up period (which lasted from 1980 to 2004 and involved 84,214 women) as compared to nonconsumers, and an 18 percent lower risk of death caused by something other than cancer or heart disease as compared with nonconsumers during follow-up. For men, this level of consumption was associated with neither a higher nor a lower risk of death during the follow-up period (which lasted from 1986 to 2004 and involved 41,736 men).

The researchers analyzed data from a pool of 84,214 women who had participated in the Nurses' Health Study and 41,736 men who had participated in the Health Professionals Follow-Up Study. Participants completed questionnaires every two to four years that included questions about how frequently they drank coffee, other dietary habits, smoking, and general health conditions. Then the researchers compared the frequency of death from any cause, death due to heart disease, and death due to cancer among people with different coffee-drinking habits.

While accounting for other risk factors, such as body size, smoking, diet, and specific diseases, the researchers found that people who drank more coffee were less likely to die during the follow-up period. This was mainly because of lower risk for heart disease deaths among coffee drinkers.

In summary, there is no conclusive evidence of any link between coffee consumption and the major diseases such as cancer, diabetes, and cardiovascular disease. On the contrary, coffee appears to have a positive impact on health. In addition to the conditions described previously, coffee provides several other health-related benefits.

Driving while sleepy results in more deaths and serious injuries than drunk driving. The US Department of Transportation considers it likely that every truck will be involved in at least one sleep-related crash during the lifetime of the vehicle and that driver fatigue is a probable factor in 20 to 40 percent of truck crashes.[24] Drinking one to two cups of coffee (about 150 mg of caffeine in total) followed by a short nap (about fifteen minutes) can significantly refresh a driver.[25]

Keeping one's eyes open and focused while driving may be a great difficulty for anyone who is sleepy. Coffee can be a great benefit in this situation, but it can go way beyond that and improve an eye condition that is much more serious. A recent Italian study suggests that drinking coffee can protect people from developing an eye tic, where an eyelid twitches uncontrollably.[26] The condition known as late-onset blepharospasm is a neurological movement disorder involving involuntary and sustained muscle contractions of the muscles around the eyes. The symptoms are often severe enough to result in functional blindness because the victim's eyelids feel as though they are clamped shut and will open only with great effort. In fact, the people have normal eyes but for periods of time are effectively blind due to their inability to open their eyelids.

Late-onset blepharospasm usually strikes people in their forties and fifties and belongs to a class of disorders known as dystonias that involve involuntary muscle contractions. Writer's cramp and musician's cramp are other examples of dystonia.

While the conclusion of this Italian study indicates that coffee consumption helps the condition, the researchers caution that it is not a cure. People who drank coffee were less likely to have late-onset blepharospasm—and the more coffee they drank, the lower their risk. Caffeine acts on receptors in a part of the brain that plays a key role in the control of eye movement.

There are a number of other conditions that respond favorably to the consumption of coffee. At this point in time, it is uncertain whether it is due to coffee's antioxidants or to its impact on the nervous system. Coffee consumption can reduce the risk of Parkinson's disease, it can reduce depression, it can speed up the recovery from liver injury, reduce the risk of gallstones, and diminish the impact of asthma.[27]

And if all that was not enough, it's hard to think of anything that can make you feel better when you get up in the morning, ready to face a new day.

3

Coffee's Expansion through Africa and the Near East

Although there are references to coffee consumption in Yemen going back as far as the late ninth century, its acceptance appeared to be very limited until close to one hundred years later. During the interim, the well-known Arab physician Abu Bakr Muhammad Bin Zakariya Ar-Razi, or simply Rhazes (852–932 CE), was the first to write down his thoughts about coffee in the year 900. Rhazes was considered one of the greatest physicians of Islam. *The Encyclopedia of Islam* refers to Rhazes as an undisputable authority of medicine up to the seventeenth century. His greatest medical work was *al-Hawi*, or *The Comprehensive Book*, which included Greek, Syrian, and early Arabic medical knowledge. Rhazes referred to the coffee bean as *bunn* and the extracted drink as *buncham*, the same designation generally used in Ethiopia.

This work on coffee was soon followed by another written by the even more celebrated Arab physician Abu Ali al-Husain Ibn Abdollah Ibn Sina, or Avicenna (930–1037 CE). He was a Persian physician and philosopher. Born near Bukhara, Persia, he had learned the Koran by the age of ten. In another six years he mastered the natural sciences and most precepts of medical theory. He began to treat the sick and soon became known as a great physician throughout the region.

Avicenna was a major interpreter of the works of Aristotle and wrote close to two hundred books on the subjects of science, religion, and philosophy. His most important works are *Shifa* (The Book of Healing) and *Al Qanun fi al-Tibb* (The Canon of Medicine), the latter being one of the most famous single works in the history of medicine. In the year 1000, using the same terms bunn and buncham for the bean and the drink, respectively, Avicenna states that coffee originated from Yemen. He describes the new drink as "hot and dry and good for the stomach."

> As to the choice thereof, that of a lemon color, light, and of good smell, is the best; the white and the heavy is naught. It is hot and dry in the first degree, and, according to others, cold in the first degree. It fortifies the members, it cleans the skin, and dries up the humidities that are under it, and gives an excellent smell to all the body.[1]

These documents appear to confirm the rather early export of coffee from the Ethiopian Highlands to Yemen. After Avicenna's references to coffee, almost nothing is written for an extended period of time. Because of this, there is still considerable controversy over the actual origins of the use of coffee in the Middle East. Some authors believe that coffee was introduced to the Middle East by Sufi clerics no earlier than the fifteenth century as a replacement for khat (*Catha edulis*), a flowering plant native to the Arabian Peninsula. Khat contains the alkaloid cathinone, which is an amphetamine-like stimulant that causes excitement and euphoria. Khat continues to be used today in countries such as Yemen, Djibouti, and Kenya. In Yemen, legend says that khat, along with coffee, was brought from Ethiopia by mystics. A significant portion of Yemen's arable land continues to be devoted to khat plantations to the point where, in order to discourage the practice, the World Health Organization classified khat as a drug of abuse that can produce mild to moderate psychological dependence.

This reference to the relatively late introduction of coffee to the Middle East is contradicted, oddly enough, by the long historical presence of an industry devoted to the production of ceramic and metal pots whose shapes have always been associated with the presence of coffee.[2] Unless additional documentation is uncovered, we can be fairly certain that coffee was consumed in the Near

East by the tenth century but may not have developed a popular following until the fifteenth century.

The most famous work on coffee was written by Sheik Abd-al-Kadir ibn Mohammad al Ansari al Jazari al Hanbali in the year 1587. Loosely titled *In Praise of Coffee*, the manuscript (now held in the Bibliotheque Nationale, Paris) is considered to be the first authentic account of the history of coffee. By the time Abd-al-Kadir's book was written, coffee had been commonly consumed in Arabia for at least a century. He attributes the discovery of the benefits of coffee to Sheik Omar, a disciple of Sheik Abou'l hasan Schadheli, the founder of Mocha, the city destined to be the major marketplace for coffee from the fifteenth to the seventeenth century.

In W. H. Ukers's book *All about Coffee* there is a translation of the story based upon the original manuscript.

In the year of Hegira 656 (C.E. 1258), the mullah Schadheli went on a pilgrimage to Mecca. Arriving at the mountain of the Emeralds (Ousab), he turned to his disciple Omar and said: "I shall die in this place. When my soul has gone forth, a veiled person will appear to you. Do not fail to execute the command which he will give you."

The venerable Schadheli being dead, Omar saw in the middle of the night a gigantic specter covered by a white veil.

"Who are you?" He asked.

The phantom drew back his veil, and Omar saw

with surprise Schadheli himself, grown ten cubits since his death. The mullah dug in the ground, and water miraculously appeared. This spirit of his teacher bade Omar fill a bowl with the water and proceed on his way and not to stop till he reached the spot where the water would stop moving.

"It is there," he added, "that a great destiny awaits you."

Omar started his journey. Arriving at Mocha in Yemen, he noticed that the water was immovable. It was here that he must stop.

The beautiful village of Mocha was then ravaged by the plague. Omar began to pray for the sick and, as the saintly man was close to Mahomet, many found themselves cured by his prayers.

The plague meanwhile progressing, the daughter of the King of Mocha fell ill and her father had her carried to the home of the dervish who cured her. But as this young princess was of rare beauty, after having cured her, the good dervish tried to carry her off. The king did not fancy this new kind of reward. Omar was driven from the city and exiled on the mountain of Ousab, with herbs for food and a cave for a home.

"Oh, Schadheli, my dear master," cried the unfortunate dervish one day; "if the things which happened to me at Mocha were destined, was it worth the trouble to give me a bowl to come here?"

To these just complaints, there was heard immediately a song of incomparable harmony and a bird of marvelous plumage came to rest in a tree. Omar sprang forward quickly toward the little bird which sang so well, but then he saw on the branches of the tree only flowers and fruit. Omar laid hands on the food, and found it delicious. Then he filled his great pockets with it and went back to his cave. As he was preparing to boil a few herbs for his dinner, the idea came to him of substituting for this sad soup, some of the harvested fruit. From it he obtained a savory and perfumed link; it was coffee.[3]

Another version of this story has Omar trying to improve the taste of the beans by roasting and steeping them in water. Omar immediately discovers how the beverage is able to refresh and enliven him. Omar returns to Mocha and is declared a hero for his discovery.

By 1300, the coffee drink—made from roasted berries, ground to powder in a mortar and pestle, and placed in boiling water—started to be popular in the region around Mocha. Within fifty years, the first Persian, Egyptian, and Turkish coffee vessels made of pottery began to be produced.

The first reliable accounts of coffee's popular acceptance throughout the Middle East refer to a date two centuries following the tale of Sheik Omar. In 1454 Sheik Gemaleddin, the mufti of Aden, returned from one of his travels to Persia and fell ill. He prepared some coffee to see whether it might improve his condition. The beverage obviously had a miraculous effect on him because not only did he recover his general health, but it also took care of his problem with headaches and invigorated him tremendously.[4] He went about promoting the consumption of coffee to his Sufi colleagues so that it would allow them to easily endure a full night of prayer without falling asleep.[5]

What is important here is coffee's broad endorsement by a very well-known and learned cleric who had made a name for himself in science and religion. Because of this, the consumption of coffee began to spread rapidly throughout Yemen and from there to other reaches of the Arab world. Coffee became a staple for all those who wished to remain alert and productive for longer periods and particularly at night. Although many were already using khat for that purpose, coffee soon replaced much of it because it had none of the drug's undesirable side effects.

With Sheik Gemaleddin's support, coffee began to be cultivated throughout Yemen, a practice that continues to this day. By the end of the fifteenth century, the Sufis introduced coffee to much of Saudi Arabia on the basis of its benefits to those who wished to spend their nights in conscious prayer. From the religious centers at Mecca and Medina, by 1510 coffee found its way to the magnificent Egyptian city of Cairo. There, a large community of Sufi dervishes originally from Yemen lived in the cloistered community. During their nights of fervent prayer, the coffee, which was kept in a large pottery vessel, was passed around for each disciple to partake. Soon, prayer and coffee drinking were inextricably associated.

It was not long before coffee made the transition from the sacred to the secular world. Gathering spots sprang up everywhere so that people congregated to drink it and passed the day in pleasant conversation. The era of the coffeehouse began.

One of the best descriptions of the early Near Eastern coffeehouses describes them as follows:

> They are commonly large halls, having their floors spread with mats, and illuminated at night by a multitude of lamps. Being the only theaters for the exercise of profane eloquence, poor scholars attend here to amuse the people. Select portions are read, e.g. the adventures of Rustan Sal, a Persian hero. Some aspire to the praise of invention, and compose tales and fables. They walk up and down as they recite, or assuming oratorial consequence, harangue upon subjects chosen by themselves.
>
> In one coffeehouse at Damascus an orator was regularly hired to tell the stories at a fixed hour; in other cases he was more directly dependent upon the taste of his hearers, as at the conclusion of his discourse, whether it had consisted of literary topics or loose and idle tales, he looked to the audience for a voluntary contribution.
>
> At Aleppo, again, there was a man with a soul above the common, who, being a person of distinction, and one that studied merely for his own pleasure, had yet gone the round of all the coffeehouses in the city to pronounce moral harangues.[6]

Thus coffeehouses immediately became centers of social life. People would sit and listen to various tales being told by professional storytellers. No doubt, a vast number of Arabian stories made the rounds in coffeehouses. Some coffeehouses had singers and others had dancers. They were the equivalent of all-hours nightclubs. From a practice that had been privy to religious clerics and their ceremonies, coffee drinking quickly became an activity all took part in. Soon, the trend spread from the coffeehouses to the homes, so that coffee could be found everywhere.

Serving coffee at home to guests became a common practice that was often augmented with very fancy coffee services made of beaten copper embellished by precious metals. Well-known artists and craftsmen applied their talents to fashion the different appliances, which were used to prepare and serve coffee. Roasters were fashioned from silver-plated brass with gold ornamentation while mortars were made from the more pedestrian bronze. The height of their art was applied to the traditional serving pots that were made from ornamented metal or, in rare cases, porcelain.

Within a short period of time, coffee could be found throughout the Near East region. From Mecca to Damascus and Cairo to Constantinople, coffee's popularity seemed limitless. However, it was not long before its ability to bring people together socially turned into a major liability.

Monarchs, religious leaders, and all other totalitarian leaders fear conspiracies. Coffeehouses had the ability to attract a great many people and stimulate them into heated debate, often political in nature. They were just the kind of venue where uprisings and traitorous meetings could take place. It was not long before the Muslim clerics began casting a wary eye upon coffee and its popularity among the people. Instead of individuals spending their hours in prayer thinking of the Great Prophet, they were enjoying themselves with secular activities in a far too democratic manner.

Coffee became a dilemma for Islam's leaders. On one hand, it was a great benefit in keeping the faithful awake and in fervent prayer during the night. On the other, they couldn't encourage people to gather together during the daytime and participate in what almost appeared to be seditious behavior. This conflict of views regarding coffee's benefits and liabilities continued for some time. Shortly after the turn of the sixteenth century, the first coffee persecutions began.

Al-Ashraf Qansuh al-Ghawri, the sultan of Egypt from 1501 to 1516, was the last of the Mamluk sultans. He established Khayr Beg as the governor of Mecca. Khayr Beg was a strong disciplinarian who was totally oblivious to the lives of his subjects. One day, while getting ready to leave the mosque after prayers, he saw a group of people in a dark shadowy corner drinking coffee in anticipation of a night of fervent prayer. The first thought that came to his mind was that they were drinking wine because they appeared to be happy. He was told that it was coffee that they were drinking, a beverage that was very popular throughout the city of Mecca. He was unaware of the habit of drinking coffee to aid in prayers and immediately proceeded to forcefully eject them all from the mosque.

In short order, he called together a representative council of physicians, clerics, judges, and leading citizens to discuss the matter. After telling them what he'd seen the previous evening, he indicated his intention to

Old Egyptian coffeehouse. (Wood-engraved illustration from George Ebers, *Egypt: Descriptive, Historical and Picturesque* [London: Cassell, Petter, Galpin and Co., 1879].)

abruptly close the coffeehouses. In effect, he called this counsel together to ensure that they endorsed his view.

Among the group that he chose as his counsel were two brothers who were also physicians. They both heartily supported Khayr Beg's views, asserting that coffee was indeed unhealthy. When it was pointed out to them that even the great Avicenna pronounced coffee fit to consume, they insisted that he had been referring to another plant entirely. Even the mufti of Aden got involved in the defense of coffee, but he was outnumbered and overruled. Khayr Beg got his way and coffee drinking was prohibited in Mecca. The governor drew up a proclamation forbidding the sale of coffee throughout the city. The coffeehouses were ordered shut and it was even forbidden to consume coffee in the home.

There was a minor revolt in the city, but it was quickly quelled with harsh justice meted out among the most outspoken lovers of coffee. However, the prohibition did not last long.

Upon hearing of this prohibition of coffee the sultan of Cairo chastised Khayr Beg, who immediately rescinded his proclamation. Not long after, the sultan found the governor in great disfavor and ordered him put to death. The two brother physicians who had so openly supported Khayr Beg quickly departed Mecca and fled to Cairo. This was not the best strategy for them because shortly thereafter they too met with the executioner, a consequence of openly insulting the Turkish emperor. Thereafter, the people of Mecca were permitted to drink their coffee in peace.

A few years later, in 1524, the grand mufti of Mecca closed the public coffeehouses supposedly because of rowdiness but permitted coffee drinking at home. However, his replacement relented and allowed coffeehouses to reopen but only under government license.

The consumption of coffee continued in Cairo without any resistance until 1534. In that year, it once more dawned on the clerics that people were spending more time in the coffeehouses around the city than in the mosques. The coffeehouses were providing a popular appeal that the houses of worship could not rival. Then, as today, fiery oratory from religious zealots had the ability to emotionally charge an issue and polarize a population. One cleric in particular stirred up emotions to a feverish pitch. Wild mobs went about the city driving patrons out of the coffeehouses and then burned them down.

However, coffee was in such great favor among a large fraction of the people that they stood their ground, thus opening the door for a much wider conflict.

Cairo's chief justice was brought in to adjudicate the matter. After a long and contentious debate, the judge decided to taste coffee for himself and immediately came down on the good side of coffee. The worthy people of Cairo, once more, could go about drinking coffee at their favorite establishments. However, it was clear that the attraction of the coffeehouses was something that religious and secular establishments would have to contend with in the future.

Constantinople was another great city that welcomed coffee. In 1517 Sultan Selim I brought coffee to the great Turkish capital right after he conquered Egypt. In Constantinople coffee drinking followed much the same historical pattern as elsewhere in the Near East. In keeping with the grandeur of the emperor's palaces and the great public buildings, Constantinople's coffeehouses, which first opened in 1554, were the epitome of elegance and fashion. Not only were they beautiful examples of Islamic architecture, replete with carpets and the great pillows on which to comfortably lean, but many of them even had decorative pools with fountains providing an attractive and tranquil atmosphere.

Coffeehouses often occupied locations that had the most picturesque views of the great city, including the magnificent panorama of the Bosporus River that flowed through it. Patrons reclined on great pillowed lounges and softly walked on richly carpeted floors. The walls often were covered with ornate coffeepots and cups of all kinds, many adorned with silver or gold inlay and precious stones.

Then, without warning, in 1570, coffee once again became the center of conflict. Again it was the Sufi clerics complaining that their mosques were empty while the coffeehouses were full. It drove them to such distraction that they declared coffee to be worse for Muslims than wine. Meetings were held and the dervishes along with other extremists vehemently pointed out that the Koran specifically forbade the eating of charcoal. Since coffee beans were roasted to the point where their skins were black, they reasoned that Muhammad had declared coffee to be a product unsuitable for consumption. Amurath III ordered the closing of all coffeehouses.

Coffee was once more officially placed on the list of forbidden substances. However, by this time, coffee consumption was so widespread that the prohibition of its consumption was almost impossible to enforce. At first the coffeehouses closed, but coffee continued to be consumed at home and at social gatherings. Soon, as a result of the persuasive powers of baksheesh (bribery), the establishments started to reopen. It did not take long before Sokolli Muhammad Pasha, also called Tawil the Tall, the famous grand vizier of Constantinople, decided that the coffeehouses would be able to provide him a handsome side revenue.[7] That put an immediate end to the persecution of coffee during his reign.

It remained that way in Constantinople for close to a century, but once more coffee came under an evil eye, this time from the government.

At the tender age of seven, Mehmed IV came to the Turkish throne after his father's murder in 1648. Schooled in religion, as sultan he prohibited alcohol and shut down all the distillers. He was wise enough to choose Constantinople's grand vizier from the famous dynasty of Koprulu to oversee his prohibition. Under Koprulu's administration, the Ottoman Empire recovered economically and militarily, annexing the greatest number of territories in its history.

In 1656, amid military operations for the island of Crete, Grand Vizier Koprulu decided to prohibit the consumption of coffee in Constantinople. It wasn't religious principles that governed his decision but rather the fear that the coffeehouses were hotbeds of sedition and could be sources of information for his enemies' spies. He was very serious about this prohibition because the punishments meted out for violations were considerable. For the first offense, the guilty party received a proper cudgeling. Anyone foolish enough to be caught a second time was tightly sown up in a leather bag and unceremoniously dumped into the Bosporus River, never to be seen alive again.

In time, however, the habit of consuming coffee slowly crept back into the lives of the Turks. Having been victorious in the battle for Crete and confident of his security, Koprulu once more permitted consumption of coffee.

As the growth of the Ottoman Empire continued, so did coffee's popularity. From Constantinople, the consumption of coffee spread to Syria, Egypt, and throughout Mesopotamia, Libya, Tunisia, and Algeria. Northward, it traveled along with the Turkish troops to Bosnia, Serbia, Moldova, and Hungary. Expansion of the Ottoman Empire was finally stopped at the gates of Vienna in 1683. By this time, however, the popularity of coffee extended beyond the region of the Near East. Coffee nearly made it to the doorstep of the Holy Roman emperor Leopold I, who reigned over a large portion of Eastern Europe, where the next stage in the saga of this beverage takes place.

Legend has it that in 1695, a pilgrim to Mecca named Baba Budan was so enamored with the taste of coffee that he was willing to risk being beheaded by smuggling some raw coffee beans out of Arabia. He hid them in his waistband and when he got back to his native India, he planted them beside his hut at Chickmaglur in the mountains of Mysore. The descendents of these plants thrived and served as the seed stock that would eventually feed much of Europe's burgeoning appetite for coffee.

4

The Conquest of Europe

The first mention of coffee by a Western writer occurs in a book of travels by German physician and biologist Leonhardt Rauwolf from Augsburg. In 1573 Rauwolf gained support from his brother-in-law, Melchior Manlich, a prominent merchant who dealt with the Levant, the area of the Eastern Mediterranean. Rauwolf began a three-year journey to the Near East in search of new plants and drugs that might be traded profitably by his brother-in-law's company. Rauwolf traveled widely throughout the Near East, managing to get as far as Persia (present-day Iran), and upon his return to Germany nine years later, he published an account of his journey.[1]

Leonhardt Rauwolf made the first recorded reference by a European to coffee and its consumption. His specific passage on coffee translates as follows:

If you would like to eat or drink something you can go to a shop [in Syria] where you sit down upon the ground on carpets with others. Among their good things, the Muslims have a very good drink which they like very much and which they call chaube [coffee]. It is black as ink and very useful in treating various ills, in particular those that involve the stomach. They are accustomed to drink it in the morning, even in public, without fear of being seen. They drink it in small porcelain cups, as hot as they can bear. They bring the cup to their lips frequently, but only take tiny sips, passing the cup on to the person sitting next to them.

They make this beverage with water and the fruit which they call bunnu, which resembles in size and color laurel berries and which is enclosed by two husks. This drink is very widespread and, as I was told, brought from the Indies. These berries have within them two yellowish seeds and appear identical to the Bunchum described by Avicenna and the Bunca of Rhazes. That is why one sees in the bazaar a great number of merchants who sell the drink or the berries. [*Bunna*, the name of the berry, still means coffee in Ethiopia and North Africa.]

Because of Constantinople's intimate trading relationship with Venice, it is most likely that Italy was the first country in Europe to experience the taste of coffee.

ITALY

Born in the republic of Venice, Prospero Alpini studied medicine at the University of Padua. Although he practiced as a physician, his interests inclined toward botany, so in 1580 he traveled to Egypt to extend his knowledge of exotic plants. On his return to Italy, he resumed practice as a physician but assumed the professorship of botany at Padua in 1593. His most famous written work is *De Plantis Aegypti liber* (The Plants of Egypt), which was published in Venice in 1592. In it he describes the coffee tree, its fruit, and a beverage the Egyptians made from it. Being a physician, Alpini spent some time discussing the medicinal qualities of coffee.

Ten years earlier, in his formal report of 1582 from Constantinople, the Venetian ambassador to the Turkish sultan described the many public establishments where people met daily to discuss business over a boiling hot black beverage.

Coffee, along with tobacco leaf, soon became an object of trade between Venice and Constantinople. Public coffeehouses began to appear in Venice in 1645. Other Italian towns followed, including Milan, Genoa, Turin, Florence, Naples, and Rome.

In Rome, coffee once again came under the jaundiced eye of religious fanaticism. The argument was classic. In 1594 Catholic clerics appealed to Pope Clement VIII, saying that Muslims were forbidden wine because it was sanctified by Christ, so to make up for it they substituted coffee. The clerics called it a black decoction from hell, and hell was where anyone who drank coffee was destined to go.

His curiosity piqued, the pope requested that coffee be brought to him in order to make a pronouncement upon it. He was so taken by the beverage's taste and aroma that he immediately blessed it as a truly Christian beverage, saying, "We will not let coffee remain the property of Satan. As Christians, our power is greater than Satan's, so we shall make coffee our own."

From that moment on, coffeehouses began to sprout all over Italy. By 1763, Venice alone had more than two hundred such establishments, many of them extraordinarily elegant. The coffeehouse tradition remains in Italy to this day, producing some of the most famous names in the world of coffee.

FRANCE

While Italy was most likely the first country in Western Europe to experience the popular consumption of coffee, France was not far behind. And what Italy did to promote the ambience and elegance of coffee, France more than made up for by eventually promoting its spread throughout the world.

The introduction of coffee in France is credited to

Jean de Thévenot (1633–1667), a natural scientist and traveler to the Near East. In his self-published book, translated as *Story of a Journey Made in the Levant*, de Thévenot describes the manner in which coffee was consumed in Turkey:

> They have another drink in ordinary use. They call it cahve and take it all hours of the day. This drink is made from a berry roasted in a pan or other utensil over the fire. They pound it into a very fine powder.
>
> When they wish to drink it, they take a boiler made expressly for the purpose, which they call an ibrik; and having filled it with water, they let it boil. When it boils, they add to about three cups of water a heaping spoonful of the powder; and when it boils, they remove it quickly from the fire, or sometimes they stir it, otherwise it would boil over, as it rises very quickly. When it has boiled up thus ten or twelve times, they pour it into porcelain cups, which they place upon a platter of painted wood and bring it to you thus boiling.
>
> One must drink it hot, but in several installments, otherwise it is not good. One takes it in little swallows for fear of burning one's self in such a fashion that in a cavekane (so they call the places where it is sold ready prepared), one hears a pleasant little musical sucking sound. There are some who mix it with small quantities of cloves and cardamom seeds; others have sugar.[2]

Because almost all spices came from Asia and the Middle East, France carried on an active trade with the Levant. French traders living in the Near East countries insisted on bringing coffee back to France when they returned home. The first commercial imports of coffee arrived at Marseilles in 1660 from Egypt. A great number of private individuals engaged in this trade and in 1671, the first coffeehouses opened in Marseille, the busiest French port engaged in Middle Eastern trade.

It wasn't long before coffee again became an item of debate. This time it was the doctors that had a go at coffee. In 1679 the medical faculty of the College of Physicians in the lovely little town of Aix-en-Provence had two of their staff bring the matter before the courts. But it was too late. The French had grown to love their coffee and the legal action was thrown out of court. On the contrary, the controversy that this action generated gave a tremendous boost to the consumption of coffee in France.

Coffee consumption in France received an unusual boost as a result of the visit of Soliman Aga Mustapha Raca, an emissary of Mehmed IV, the sultan of the Ottoman Empire, who was sent as an official ambassador to the court of King Louis XIV in November 1669. Soliman's visit was intended to restore full diplomatic ties between France and Turkey as a means of keeping the Hapsburg monarchy, which controlled the Austrian Empire, in check. In order to try and establish a pecking order, Louis XIV made it clear that he was in no hurry to see the emissary. Not someone to be put off, Soliman immediately purchased a grand house in Paris and began to entertain the city's upper classes.

His palatial home was decked out in the most elegant Eastern style, including tiled arches and sumptuous brocaded pillows spread out over luxurious silk carpets. His lavish receptions featured splendid meals flavored with exotic spices and always concluded with Turkish coffee. The Parisians flocked to his door, not wanting to miss any opportunity to be in his company. It was even fashionable to come clad in dressing gowns and silk turbans. More important, coffee took hold instantly and became a highly sought-after beverage.

Within two years of Soliman Aga Mustapha Raca's visit, elegant coffeehouses called *cabarets a café*—as elegant as those found in the capitals of the Near East—began to cater to the French. In order to complement the decor of these establishments, French artisans applied their decorative arts to the utensils required for the preparation and consumption of coffee.

ENGLAND

Although there were numerous English travelers to the Near East from the time of the first Crusades, the first mention of coffee in England came from a translation of a Dutch travelogue titled *Linschoten's Travels*, published in 1598. This extraordinary work was partly a discourse on sailing, commercial possibilities, and Near Eastern geography.

Linschoten compared the Turkish drinking of coffee to the Japanese habit of drinking tea and described it as follows:

> The Turks hold almost the same manner of drinking of their Chaona, which they make of certain fruit, which is like unto the Bakekaer and by the Egyptians called Bon or Ban: They take of this fruit one pound and a half, and roast them a little in the fire and then seith them in twenty pounds of water, till the half be consumed away: This drink they take every morning fasting in their chambers, out of an earthen pot, being veri hot, as we do here drink aquacompositoria in the morning: and they say that it strengtheneth and maketh them warm, breaketh wind, and openeth any stopping.

In his book *Travels and Adventure*, published in 1603, seafaring captain John Smith spoke highly of Turkish coffee. Not only did he enlighten his fellow Englishmen, but when he sailed off to the New World to become the governor of Virginia, he carried with him the first knowledge of the black beverage. This is the same Captain Smith who was saved from certain death at the hands of native Indians by the intervention of young Pocahontas.

At the turn of the fifteenth century, William Biddulph was a Protestant clergyman who lived in the Ottoman Empire for eight years and served as a chaplain in Aleppo, Syria. Self-absorbed and generally disagreeable, he enjoyed the respect his clerical office received from his fellow Englishmen. His book first published in 1609, *The Travels of Certaine Englishmen into Africa, Asia, Troy, Bythinia, Thracia, and to the Blacke Sea*, contains this description of Turkish coffeehouses:

> Their most common drinke is Coffa, which is a blacke kinde of drinke, made of a kind of Pulse like Pease, called Coaua; which being grownd in the Mill, and boiled in water, they drinke it as hot as they can suffer it; which they finde to agree very well with them against their crudities, and feeding on hearbs and rawe meates.
>
> It is accounted a great curtesie amongst them to give on to their friends when they come to visit them, a Fin-ion or Scudella of Coffa, which is more holesome than toothsome, for it causeth good concoction, and driveth away drowsiness.
>
> Their Coffa houses are more common than Alehouses in England; but they use not so much to sit in the houses, as on benches on both sides the streets, neere unto a Coffa house, that every man with his Fin-ionful; which being smoking hot, they use to put it to their Noses & Eares, and then sup it off by leasure, being full of idle and Ale-house talke whiles they are amongst themselves drinking it; if there be any news, it is talked of there.

Even the venerable Lord Francis Bacon (1561–1626), baron of Verulam, weighed in on the subject in his *Sylva Sylvarum* published in 1627, a year after his death:

Their moſt common drinke is Coffa, which Coffa.
is a blacke kind of drinke made of a kind of Pulſe like Peaſe,
called Coaua; which being ground in the mill, and boiled in
water, they drinke it as hot as they can ſuffer it; which they
find to agrée very well with them againſt their crudities and
féeding on hearbs and rawe meates.

It is accounted a great curteſie amongſt them to giue vnto
their freends when they come to viſit them, a Fin-ion or Scudeb
la of Coffa, which is more holeſome than toothſome, for it cau-
ſeth good concoction, and driueth away drowſinesse.

Their Coffa houſes are more common than Ale-houſes in
England; but they vſe not ſo much to ſit in the houſes as on
benches on both ſides the ſtréets néere vnto a Coffa houſe, euery
man with his Fin-ion ful; which being ſmoking hot, they vſe to
put it to their noſes & eares, and then ſup it off by leaſure, being
full of idle and Ale-houſe talke whiles they are amongſt them-
ſelues drinking of it; if there be any news, it is talked of there.

Biddulph text. (From William Biddulph, *The Travels of
Certaine Englishmen into Africa, Asia, Troy, Bythinia,
Thracia, and to the Blacke Sea* [London: W. Aspley, 1609].)

They have in Turkey a drink called coffa made of a
berry of the same name, as black as soot, and of a
strong scent, but not aromatical; which they take,
beaten into powder, in water as hot as they can drink it:
and they take it, and sit at it in their coffa-houses, which
are like our taverns. This drink comforteth the brain
and heart, and helpeth digestion. Certainly this berry
coffa, the root and leaf betel, the leaf tobacco, and the

tear of poppy (opium) of which the Turks are great takers (supposing it expelleth all fear), do all condense the spirits and make them strong and alegar. But it seemeth they were taken after several manners; for coffa and opium are taken down, tobacco but in smoke, and betel is but champed in the mouth with a little lime.

It is interesting to note that the term *coffa*, which was clearly taken from the Near East and initially used in England, was changed to *coffee* by the mid-eighteenth century, as can be seen from an edition in a collection of Bacon's works printed in 1753. Here is a scan of the pertinent paragraph:

Cent. VIII.   N A T U R A L   H I S T O R Y.

Experiment solitary touching medicines that condense and relieve the spirits.

738. They have in Turkey a drink called coffee, made of a berry of the same name, as black as soot, and of a strong scent, but not aromatical; which they take, beaten into powder, in water, as hot as they can drink it: and they take it, and sit at it in their coffee-houses, which are like our taverns. This drink comforteth the brain and heart, and helpeth digestion. Certainly this berry coffee, the root and leaf betle, the leaf tobacco, and the tear of poppy *(opium)* of which the Turks are great takers (supposing it expelleth all fear) do all condense the spirits, and make them strong and aleger. But it seemeth they are taken after several manners; for coffee and *opium* are taken down, tobacco but in smoak, and betle is but champed in the mouth with a little lime. It is like there are more of them, if they were well found out, and well corrected. *Quaere* of henbane-seed, of mandrake; of saffron, root and flower; of *folium indicum*; of ambergreece; of the *Assyrian amomum*, if it may be had; and of the scarlet powder, which they call *kermes*; and (generally) of all such things as do inebriate and provoke sleep. Note, that tobacco is not taken in root or seed, which are more forcible ever than leaves.

Francis Bacon text.

Bacon's contemporary Robert Burton (1577–1640) made the following reference to coffee in his 1632 book, *The Anatomy of Melancholy*, a work he completed largely to avoid suffering from chronic melancholy. Burton had a habit of mimicking Bacon in many of his writings, as can be seen from this description of coffee.

> The Turkes have a drinke called coffa (for they use the wine), so named of a berry as blacke as soot and as bitter (like that blacke drinke which was in use amongst the Lacedemonians and perhaps the same), which they sip still of, and sup as warme as they can suffer; they spend much time in those coffa-houses which are somewhat like our Ale-houses or Taverns, and there they sit, chatting and drinking, to drive away the time, and to be merry together, because they find, by experience, that kinde of drinke so used, helpeth digestion and procureth alacrity.

Sir Henry Blount (1602–1682) was one of England's more well-known travelers. In May 1634, on a Venetian galley he embarked on his famous trip to be recorded in his best-selling book *A Voyage into the Levant*, published two years later. Blount proceeded to sail down the Adriatic coast and eventually entered Bosnia, and from there took a nine-day journey to Sarajevo. He then traveled with Turkish troops heading into the war with Austria and stopped at Belgrade, on the banks of the Danube. From there he traveled to Constantinople, completing a land journey of fifteen hundred miles in fifty-two days—an amazing feat. He stayed for only five days and immediately took passage with the Turkish fleet headed for Egypt. Basing himself in Alexandria, he made a number of whirlwind tours to the interior of Egypt and before too long, he headed back home via Sicily, Naples, Rome, Florence, and, of course, Venice.

Blount's interest in the Near East was more scientific and commercial than cultural. He felt a great part of his mission was to bring commercial benefits to Britain. During the period of his travels, the Ottoman Empire was at the peak of its power and magnificence. He assiduously took notes on everything he observed and brought the art of travelogue writing to extraordinary new heights.

> They have another drink not good at meat, called Cauphe, made of a Berry as big as a small Bean, dried in a Furnace, and beat to Pouder, of a Soot-colour, in taste a little bitterish, that they seeth and drink as hot as may be endured: It is good all hours of the day, but especially morning and evening, when to that purpose, they entertain themselves two or three hours in Cauphe-houses, which in all Turkeys abound more than Inns and Ale-houses with us; it is thought to be the old black broth use so much by the Lacedemonians, and dryeth ill Humours in the stomach, comforteth the Brain, never causeth Drunkenness or any other Surfeit and is a harmless entertainment of good Fellowship; for there upon Scaffolds half a yard high,

and covered with Mats, they sit Cross-leg'd after the Turkish manner, many times two or threes hundred together, talking, and likely with some poor musick passing up and down.

One of the most interesting stories of the time concerns William Harvey, easily the foremost physician of his time. Even though some elements regarding the circulation of the blood in humans were partially known, it was Harvey who completely elucidated the subject and put it squarely on the map with his 1628 treatise, *An Anatomical Exercise on the Motion of the Heart and Blood in Animals*. Harvey studied at one of the most famous medical schools in the world, the University of Padua. While there, he discovered coffee drinking and found that it provided him the energy and mental clarity to conduct his studies tirelessly. It was not long before he became obsessed with coffee and served as one of its greatest proponents throughout his life. He constantly praised its therapeutic values and considered it a panacea for sloth and drunkenness. He urged his colleagues to give up beer and wine so that they might more effectively pursue their professions.

His habit of drinking coffee was so well known that it was even mentioned in John Aubrey's famous book, *Brief Lives*.

I remember he was wont to drinke Coffee; which he and his brother Eliab did, before Coffee-houses were in fashion in London.[3]

According to Anthony Wood, author of the famous work *Athenae Oxonienses*, the first coffeehouse in England was opened in 1650 in Oxford.

> In 1650 Jacob, a Jew, opened a Coffee House at the Angel in the parish of St. Peter in the East, Oxen, and there it was drunk by some who delighted in novelties.[4]

Coffee quickly caught on among the local students. As a result of its popularity, the students at Oxford persuaded a local apothecary named Arthur Tillyard to open up a shop for the express purpose of preparing and selling coffee to the students. This establishment opened in 1655 under the name of the Oxford Coffee Club. Within a short period, some of Oxford's leading scientists and their students regularly gathered to discuss their research and theories over coffee. Among the most famous patrons was Britain's most renowned chemist, Sir Robert Boyle. The scientific company of coffee drinkers grew and eventually became the world-famous Royal Society, a fraternity based on the quality of the candidates' scientific output without prejudicial regard to politics, religion, or social standing—and all because of coffee.

In the meantime, London's first coffeehouse was opened by Pasqua Rosée in 1652 in St. Michael's Alley, Cornhill, London. A native of Turkey, Rosée, who was used to brewing coffee, was brought to London by a Near Eastern trader, Daniel Edwards. Edwards's colleagues were so taken by the brew that he encouraged Rosée to open the city's first coffeehouse. In a short period of time several other coffeehouses were established throughout the city and these establishments soon became centers of London's social life. Jacob, who opened the original coffeehouse at Oxford, eventually moved to London, where he opened yet another coffeehouse.

NETHERLANDS

From the time of its secession from the Holy Roman Empire, the tiny country of the Netherlands became an acknowledged world power through the strength of its merchant shipping and the military might of its navy. These strengths led to an extended period of economic, scientific, and cultural growth—all based on Netherlands' flair for international trade.

Because of their trading merchants who operated throughout the Orient, the Dutch were familiar with coffee. Soon after the establishment of the Dutch East India Company, the first shipment of coffee arrived from Mocha in 1616, brought to the Netherlands by trader Pieter Van dan Broecke. The first large shipment was offered for public sale in Amsterdam in 1640 by the Dutch merchant Wurffbain. Coffee drinking quickly became a Dutch habit.

When the Dutch navy succeeded in driving the Portuguese out of Ceylon in 1658, they began the cultivation of coffee based on the plants originally brought to Ceylon by Arabs. It took some time, but commercial-sized shipments began arriving for auction in Amsterdam.

Once they had an understanding of its agronomic requirements, the resourceful Dutch shipped seedlings to the island of Java in Indonesia and developed major coffee plantations there in 1696. Within ten years, a trial shipment of coffee from Batavia (present-day Jakarta) arrived. In this shipment was a plant destined for Amsterdam's botanical gardens. This seemingly insignificant plant was destined for great things, but more on that later.

The first commercial shipments from Java (almost nine hundred pounds) arrived in Amsterdam in 1711 and cost about fifty cents a pound, which comes to twenty to thirty dollars in today's currency. In the process of becoming a highly valued commodity of trade, coffee also brought out the negative side of Holland's ambitions to remain a major player in international trade. While the genteel citizens of Amsterdam and Utrecht drank coffee in their elegant surroundings, some of their brothers and uncles assumed the role of cruel overseers of coffee cultivation in Java, instituting a system of forced labor on the plantations. So ingrained and pervasive was this forced labor system of coffee cultivation that it continued long after all other forms of forced labor were outlawed.

As in all other countries, the local coffeehouse became a popular institution—a custom that survives to the present day.

VIENNA

The introduction of coffee to Vienna places it squarely in the middle of great historical events.

At its peak, the Holy Roman Empire encompassed the territories of Germany, Austria, Switzerland, Liechtenstein, Luxembourg, the Czech Republic, Slovenia, Belgium, and the Netherlands, as well as large parts of modern Poland, France, and Italy. Powerful as it was, the empire's rulers stood in great fear of the Turkish onslaught. The Holy Roman emperor Leopold I had been made aware of the Turkish army's intention to attack Vienna. In order to enhance his prestige at the Ottoman court, Grand Vizier Kara Mustapha Pasha began the siege of Vienna on July 14, 1683, with an army of approximately 140,000 men (more than half of whom were inexperienced).

Leopold I immediately fled to the city of Linz to negotiate with the king of Poland, Jan III Sobieski, asking him to assemble a force large enough to deal with Kara Mustafa. In the meantime the residents of Vienna were in panic as a result of the continuous fusillade of cannon fire from the Turks. By August, the dead and wounded lay dying in the streets, the hospitals too over-crowded to accommodate them. Dysentery broke out, adding to the great city's misery. Everyone knew that if Vienna fell, it would spell the beginning of the end for the Holy Roman Empire.

Although a great number of allied forces were positioned outside of Vienna, they were unable to coordinate with the forces inside the walls of the city. At that moment, an unlikely hero, Franz George Kolschitzky, came to the rescue. Born in Galicia, Poland, Kolschitzky had been a Turkish interpreter and had lived many years among the Turks. He offered to serve as the courier of letters between the chief of Vienna's armed forces and the military leaders of the relief armies outside of the city. To do this, he had to pass through Turkish lines.

In the middle of August, Kolschitzky, dressed in full Turkish garb, crossed the Danube, walked through the endless line of tents of the besieging Turkish army, and reached the duke of Lorraine's forces. Kolschitzky made the round-trip several times over the next few weeks and did much to reinvigorate the city's lagging morale in the process.

Finally, the allied German and Polish armies were ready to attack the Turks and relieve Vienna   one of the most decisive and dramatic moments in European history. Jan III Sobieski planned to attack on the thirteenth of September, but Kolschitzky's reports indicated that the Turkish deployments were poorly arranged, so he ordered a full attack on September 12 despite being vastly outnumbered. Kara Mustafa Pasha had entrusted the defense of his rear to the khan of Crimea and thirty thousand Tartars who were under his command.

The decisive battle began at 6 a.m. with an initial attack against the Turkish positions to the north of the city. The fierce battle carried on throughout the day and was concluded with a magnificent attack by Sobieski leading the mounted heavy lancers, the famed "Winged Hussars," against the main Turkish force at 6 o'clock in the evening. As a result of Sobieski's superior generalship, Kara Mustafa and the Turks were outmaneuvered and fled the field, leaving a treasure of livestock, grain, musical instruments, cannons, gold, and sacks and sacks of coffee. That twelve-hour battle changed the course of history and shaped the outcome of the entire war. It was the beginning of the end of the Ottoman Empire. Three months later on December 25, 1683, Kara Mustafa Pasha was taken into Belgrade by the commander of the Janissaries, who had him strangled and decapitated in the traditional method used for the Ottoman Empire's highest officials.

Much of the booty left on the field of battle was totally unfamiliar to the Christians of Vienna. When they came across the great number of sacks of coffee, they were inclined to dump them into the Danube. Kolschitzky, who was fully familiar with the beverage, jumped forward and asked for them. The Viennese were so grateful for his services during the campaign that they readily acquiesced to his request.

Kolschitzky was also presented with a house as an additional reward and, in short order, opened up the Blue Bottle, the first establishment in Vienna to serve coffee. To this day, Kolschitzky is considered the patron saint of coffee in Vienna. A famous painting of Kolschitzky's café by Franz Schams hangs in the boardroom of the renowned Viennese Julius Meinl Coffee Company. There is also a monument to him on the corner of Favoritenstrasse and a street named after him, Kolschitzkygassse.

The consumption of coffee in Vienna became very popular. Coffeehouses sprung up around the city and became a mainstay of its character to this day. Vienna has some of the most elegant coffeehouses in Europe and the world. Viennese coffee—that superb blend of coffee, cream, and chocolate—is rich, decadent, and a delicious reminder of the city's place in the history of coffee.

GERMANY

As mentioned earlier, Leonhardt Rauwolf traveled to Syria in 1573 and nine years later wrote about his experiences, thus becoming the first European to mention coffee in print. Despite that, it took close to a century before coffee drinking was introduced to Germany, and even then it was an Englishman who opened the first coffeehouse in Hamburg in 1679. In short order, all the other major German cities opened coffeehouses: Leipzig in 1694, Nuremberg in 1696, Stuttgart in 1712, and Berlin in 1721.

But coffee soon met with opposition once again. Frederick the Great was upset when he found out how much foreign currency was being spent on importing coffee beans. He tried to institute a government monopoly on roasting, but this didn't last long. When the poor complained that coffee was too expensive, they were told it was best not to drink it because it would leave them sterile. In response, Bach wrote his "Coffee Cantata" in 1732 as a protest and as a reminder of how much the public loved coffee.

Frederick went much further in September 1777 when he issued a manifesto on coffee and beer, declaring:

> It is disgusting to notice the increase in the quantity of coffee used by my subjects, and the amount of money that goes out of the country in consequence. Everybody is using coffee. If possible this must be prevented. My people must drink beer. His Majesty was brought up on beer, and so were his ancestors, and his officers. Many battles have been fought and won by soldiers nourished on beer; and the King does not believe that coffee-drinking soldiers can be depended upon to endure hardship or to beat his enemies in case of the occurrence of another war.

This pronouncement was successful and the lower-class citizens stopped demanding coffee for a period and returned to beer. But Frederick observed that, as the rich continued to drink coffee, the poor and middle class began demanding it again. He thus decided to make coffee roasting a privilege limited to the upper classes with the *Déclaration du Roi concernant la vente du café brûlé*, or the King's Declaration concerning the Law of Roasted Coffee, issued in 1781.

In order to enforce the law, the government employed retired soldiers to go among the people sniffing for the aroma of roasting coffee. People caught in the act were heavily fined and the soldiers were paid one quarter of the fines collected—a considerable incentive. Soon these roasted coffee sniffers were among the most disliked people in Germany.

Following in Frederick's footsteps, the bishop of Münster issued a similar manifesto in 1784:

> To our great displeasure, we have learned that in our Duchy of Westphalia the misuse of the coffee beverage has become so extended that to counteract the evil we command that four weeks after the publication of this decree no one shall sell coffee roasted or not roasted under a fine of one hundred florins, or two years in prison, for each offense.
>
> Every coffee-roasting and coffee-serving place shall be closed, and dealers and hotel-keepers are to get rid of their coffee supplies in four weeks. It is only

permitted to obtain from the outside coffee for one's own consumption in lots of fifty pounds. House fathers and mothers shall not allow their work people, especially their washing and ironing women, to prepare coffee, or to allow it in any manner under a penalty of one hundred florins.

All officials and government employees, to avoid a penalty of one hundred gold florins, are called upon to closely follow and keep a watchful eye over this decree. To the one who reports such persons as act contrary to this decree shall be granted one-half of the said money fine with absolute silence as to his name.

Once more, the coffee sniffers became the enemy of the common citizen. Ultimately, the scheme failed as did others intended to unfairly tax the German citizens on what was soon to become one of their favorite beverages.

5

Coffee Makes Its Way to the New World

Although Captain John Smith may have brought the knowledge of coffee to North America, no records of the commodity appeared in the colonies until 1670. Coffeehouses soon appeared, patterned after their English counterparts. Because coffee and tea were such expensive commodities in the colony, the common infusions that were consumed as beverages were often made from other herbs, flowers, and grasses that were locally available.

Back in England, starting at the latter half of the seventeenth century, as a result of the aggressive marketing efforts of the British East India Company, tea became the beverage of choice. The North American colonies followed suit, but King George decided to institute the Stamp Act of 1765, which made tea more expensive and upset the colonists enough that they stopped buying other English goods. Although the tea tax was temporarily repealed, the colonists continued to resist purchasing British goods and changed the history of the world by dumping a shipment of tea into Boston Harbor. In a short period of time, drinking coffee became more popular than tea, the latter being considered an unpatriotic beverage.

Coffee began being served in the taverns and inns throughout New England. The first proper coffeehouses appeared in Boston and were named in a similar fashion to the local taverns, such as the King's Head, the Indian Queen, the Green Dragon, and so on. Strangely enough, because of the military and class distinctions that characterized early colonial America, coffeehouses in Boston catered to a specific clientele. The Indian Queen coffeehouse was a favorite of British military officers, while the King's Head was the haunt of the colonial upper class. An exception was the Green Dragon coffeehouse, an institution that figured in almost all the important affairs of Boston from 1697 to 1832. Here you could find pompous crown officers, the upper classes, and governing politicians, mixing it all up with ragtag revolutionaries.

Daniel Webster wrote:

> . . . It was under the circumstances, and at this crisis, that the tradesmen of the town of Boston, in January, 1788, assembled at the Green Dragon Tavern, the place where the Whigs of the Revolution, in its early

stages, had been accustomed to assemble. . . . These resolutions were carried to the Boston delegates in the convention, and placed in the hands of Samuel Adams. That great and distinguished friend of American liberty, it was feared, might have doubts about the new Constitution. Naturally cautious and sagacious, it was apprehended he might fear the practicability, or the safety, of a general government. He received the resolutions from the hands of Paul Revere, a brass founder by occupation, a man of sense and character, and of high public spirit, whom the mechanics of Boston ought never to forget. 'How many mechanics,' said Mr. Adams, 'were at the Green Dragon when these resolutions were passed?' 'More Sir,' was the reply, 'than the Green Dragon could hold.'[1]

It is no wonder that Daniel Webster considered the Green Dragon the "headquarters of the Revolution."

New York has a different story. It is thought that the original Dutch founders of New Amsterdam may have been the first to introduce coffee to the city. Once the British took over New York, however, English drinking habits quickly prevailed. The first infusion to be introduced was tea, but this was soon followed by coffee, which quickly became a favorite of the hardworking colonists. As in Boston, the coffeehouses did not serve as centers of intellectual endeavor but focused more on the needs of specific classes and the individual trades. In some cases, coffeehouses even served as the local courtrooms.

In Philadelphia, the initial introduction of coffee is attributed to William Penn, the colony's founder. There, as in New York and Boston, coffeehouses served the more prosaic purpose of public meeting places.

The most heroic tale of coffee and its introduction to the New World involves the efforts of Captain Gabriel Mathieu de Clieu, a young French naval officer.

As previously noted, it was the enterprising spirit of the Dutch that resulted in the huge success of Javanese coffee production. While they were occupied with spreading the propagation of coffee throughout the Indonesian archipelago (Sumatra, Bali, Timor, etc.), their trade rivals, the French, were quietly making plans to introduce coffee into their colonies. In 1706 the Dutch made a small shipment of coffee beans from their plantations in Java to Amsterdam. Together with the shipment of beans was a young coffee tree destined for the botanical gardens in that same city. The tree was carefully tended to and flourished. Several plants were propagated from its seeds and distributed to botanical gardens around Europe. Unfortunately, all attempts to introduce coffee to the botanical gardens of Paris failed, making France one of the few countries in Europe that did not have a specimen of this exotic new plant.

In 1714, as a result of negotiations between the French government and the city of Amsterdam, the city's burgomeister graciously offered to give King Louis XIV of France a healthy direct descendant of the original tree that was sent from Java. The tree was delivered to Marly-le-Roi, Louis's supposedly simple country retreat that ended up costing more than Versailles. Wisely, the young king immediately had it planted in a greenhouse at the Jardin des Plantes, the Royal Garden, in Paris. It was this tree that ended up being the genetic parent of most of the coffee found in Latin America.

The French were very eager to get into the coffee business. Their agents purchased seeds and trees on the black market and quietly had them shipped to the island of Île Bourbon (now Réunion), off the east coast of Africa. The seeds failed to vigorously take hold, and all but one of the trees eventually died out. In spite of this, several thousand seeds from that one tree were planted, and in 1720, a plantation was finally established there. Coffee was then considered such a strategic crop that France reserved the death penalty for anyone found illegally trading seeds or destroying a tree.

Still wanting to establish coffee in their Caribbean colonies, seeds from the Jardin des Plantes tree were sent to the French Antilles on two occasions, but they never took root.

The eventual success of the French in establishing coffee production in their Caribbean colonies was the result of the heroic efforts of a young French naval officer serving on the island of Martinique. His name was Gabriel Mathieu de Clieu.

On a trip back to France, he thought of the idea of

introducing coffee to the island of Martinique. He had heard of the huge plantations of coffee on the island of Java in Indonesia and knew from his own experience in Paris that coffee was becoming very popular. He wanted desperately to put France into the coffee production business. Unfortunately the only plants he knew of were those in the Royal Gardens in Paris. The problem was that he did not have access to the healthy seedlings that were offspring of the original tree in the Jardin des Plantes, because they were jealously guarded by Monsieur Jussieu, the royal botanist who repeatedly refused de Clieu's many written requests.

He enlisted the assistance of Monsieur de Chirac, the physician of Louis XV. De Chirac imposed his courtly authority upon Jussieu, who finally relented and allowed de Clieu to have two seedlings, which he immediately sent to the port of Rochefort. They were kept there until de Clieu was ready to embark for Martinique. On November 20, 1723, he finally set sail for Martinique on the merchant ship *Dromedary*.

Having vowed to himself that, upon his honor, his little plant would reach his destination safely, de Clieu guarded his plants with utmost care. The potted seedlings were kept under a glass enclosure so they might better hold the heat and moisture while absorbing the sunlight. It also protected the plants against unwanted insects that may have found their way on board. Unfortunately there was far more to worry about than insects.

There was another individual aboard the *Dromedary* who apparently knew what de Clieu was up to. He did his utmost to steal the seedlings and take the glory of being the first to bring coffee to the New World. In an article written for the French magazine *L'Année Littéraire*, de Clieu wrote, "It is useless to recount in detail the infinite care that I was obliged to bestow upon this delicate plant during our long voyage, and the difficulties I had in saving it from the hands of a man who, basely jealous of the joy I was about to taste through being of service to my country, and being unable to get this coffee plant away from me, tore off a branch." (In another account, this oafish seaman had a strong Dutch accent, leading us to believe that the government of the Netherlands may have been behind this attempt to steal the plant away from de Clieu—a credible theory considering the Dutch government's fierce attempts at maintaining a monopoly over coffee production.)[2]

It's hard to imagine the dynamics aboard the tiny ship: a long voyage with few passengers on board and one of them so determined to steal the property of another that he was even able to tear a small branch off of the seedling. It is possible they came to blows over de Clieu's little treasure. Nevertheless, de Clieu prevailed and managed to save the plants from total destruction. (There's also some controversy as to whether there were one or two seedlings.)

The *Dromedary* was a merchant ship not built for

speed or skirmishing with pirates. Nonetheless, they managed to elude capture by one of the many Tunisian pirate ships that routinely forged the waters of the Mediterranean near the Straits of Gibraltar. As soon as the passengers heaved a sigh of relief at their luck in avoiding the pirates, the ship encountered a vicious storm navigating through the treacherous waters of the straits. The heavy seas threatened to capsize the small ship, but their luck held.

When they finished plying their way through the heavy seas, the *Dromedary* exited the Mediterranean and headed out into the Atlantic. After a short period, it sailed into tropical waters where the *Dromedary* more than lived up to her name. Beset by the calm of the Doldrums, the *Dromedary* crept along, slow as a camel. The Doldrums—that low-pressure area on either side of the equator where the prevailing winds are exceedingly calm—were always considered the most dangerous part of any transoceanic voyage for sailing ships. Without the winds to push them along, they had no means of propelling their craft forward.

Trapped in the region just north of the equator and smack in the middle of the two trade wind streams, sailors could be stuck in the Doldrums for weeks. The rising hot equatorial air took their breath away and sucked the moisture out of everything. Adhering to standard protocol for all ships caught in this predicament, the *Dromedary*'s captain ordered that all water be carefully rationed.

In order to save his seedlings and his honor, de Clieu used most of his precious water ration to keep his seedlings alive. The total absence of wind forced de Clieu to do without a full ration of water for more than a month. Finally, the *Dromedary* landed in Martinique and de Clieu disembarked, proudly holding his healthy little seedling.

De Clieu planted the seedling on his estate over-looking the sea in the Pecheur region of Martinique. There, the seedling flourished and multiplied with extra-ordinary rapidity. He distributed seeds of the original plant to those individuals whom he trusted and thus spread its agriculture quickly. He continued to distribute the seeds and in his quest to extend the cultivation of coffee widely he was aided by a freak streak of nature. Either a hurricane blew through or a volcano erupted, which was followed by continuous rain inundating the island's cocoa plantations. This created the conditions for the widespread dissemination of coffee beans, which took root in Martinique and were quickly followed in Guadeloupe, Santo Domingo, and other islands close by. In less than a decade, there were close to 20 million coffee trees growing in Martinique alone.

Both the French and the Dutch began to grow coffee on the northeast coast of South America. The Brazilians, who had vast lands to devote to agriculture, were also interested in growing coffee, but the seeds and seedlings were guarded so jealously by both the Dutch and the

French that it was impossible to get hold of any planting material. Their chance came when French and Dutch Guiana (Surinam) began to dispute the precise border that divided the two countries. In 1727 both the French and the Dutch did not want their dispute to break out into military conflict for fear that it might cut back on their production, so they asked Brazil to intervene and negotiate the final border.

The Brazilians sent a well-known army colonel named Francisco de Melo Palheta, who was also famous for exploring large areas of Brazil. On top of that, he happened to be an incorrigible ladies' man. In the midst of the negotiations and examinations of maps, surveys, and claims, he wasted no time in seducing the wife of the governor of French Guiana, Madame d'Orvilliers. Once Palheta helped resolve the dispute, the French governor held a banquet in his honor. The wife of the governor, obviously grateful for the attention Palheta bestowed upon her, offered him a grand bouquet of flowers. Hidden among the various garden flowers were seeds and cuttings of the coffee plant. Palheta brought these back to Brazil with him and eventually changed the world of coffee production forever.

It was not long before Brazil became the world's largest producer of coffee, a situation that has remained to this day.

6

The Dark Side of the Coffee Trade

The institution of slavery is as old as civilization. The frequent and brutal wars that were characteristic of early civilizations created the first supply of slaves—the conquered peoples who had their freedom taken away and were forced to labor for the benefit of the victors. Of course, there were other methods by which individuals could be enslaved such as through kidnapping or piracy. The common characteristic that is germane to all forms of slavery was that the slaves were put into hard labor to enrich the slave owners.

Slavery was an accepted fact of life in the Middle East from before the time of Muhammad. The Muslim holy book, the Koran, offers no guidance against this practice. On the contrary, it takes slavery for granted and recommends that slaves, particularly females, should be treated well. The Christian Gospels are hardly any better since they do not mention slaves at all even though they were common along with indentured servants in the households of the wealthy.

Before coffee fell into the hands of the Europeans, it was a crop that was generally grown by small independent farmers throughout the Levant, much in the same way as all other crops. However, after the Portuguese first landed on the west coast of Africa and teamed up with the Arab slave traders, who had been supplying labor to the trans-Sahara caravans, the slave trade became an active part of European life. It became a goal of European colonial powers to produce coffee in foreign lands through the use of slave or indentured labor. Coffee cultivation came to represent the unbridled ambitions of a class of men who would stop at nothing to enrich themselves. This was not so much a reflection of one particular colonial power or another, but rather the representation of a small class of wealthy entrepreneurs and bankers in each of these countries who saw market opportunities for coffee as well as the potential for extreme exploitation of primitive labor. They quickly maneuvered in order to become politically empowered to take advantage of the opportunity.

These were the men of the various East Indies trading companies that were established in the Netherlands, England, France, Spain, and Portugal. Having learned from the exploits of the great navigators that the world was round and therefore finite, these men set about grabbing as much wealth and resources they could get, given the limited technology of the times. Once established by the statutes of their native countries, the trading companies devised a simple strategy. Seize as much land as possible, force slaves or indentured peasants to produce high-value crops, then sell the commodities in the lucrative European markets and bank or reinvest the cash in similar schemes.

It did not matter whether the crop was coffee, tea, cocoa, or sugar. If the people cultivating the crops could be subjugated either by guile, corruption, or brute force, they could be easily put to work and enrich their captors. Slave life was condemnation to an existence of unimaginable grief, systematically applied and kept in place for generations to prevent any changes in the status quo. Unfortunately, in some parts of the world, this form of exploitation continues through today.

Among the first to employ slavery in the coffee business were the Dutch. At the turn of the seventeenth century, there was a pan-European scramble to achieve a monopoly on the Oriental spice trade. Following the extraordinary seafaring exploits of the great explorers such as Columbus, Magellan, and Vasco da Gama, the Portuguese, Spanish, English, and Dutch all wanted to control spices that began to flow in from the East. The Portuguese had a head start in Malacca in the early part of the sixteenth century. They were not particularly efficient traders and their poor management of the supply chain opened up opportunities for others. The first Dutch attempt to break the Portuguese hold on the spice trade was a total commercial success.

In the year 1602 an influential group of Dutch merchants and shipping magnates came together to form the United East India Company (*Vereenigde Oost-Indische Companie*, or VOC). The Dutch government empowered VOC to maintain a fighting force, build fortifications, and negotiate treaties with the rulers of Asian states. Within a year of its founding, the United East India Company established its first prominent trading post in Java, Indonesia, soon to be followed by another in Jayakarta, Batavia—present-day Jakarta.

In 1696 the first trial shipment of coffee seedlings was sent to Java, but they did not take root due to flooding. A second shipment of seedlings was sent three years later, in 1699. They successfully took hold and the new coffee kingdom of Java came into being. It remains a major producer of coffee through today, and the term *java* has been synonymous with coffee for centuries.

Once coffee cultivation had become established in Java, the Dutch imposed forced coffee cultivation in West Java. In order to maximize their revenues, the Dutch colonial government implemented a series of policies termed the "cultivation system," which forced Indonesian farmers to grow a quota of commercially tradable crops such as coffee instead of growing staple foods such as rice. They made contracts with local regents who forced their subjects to produce the required amounts of coffee. At the same time, the government implemented a tax collection system where the collecting agents were paid by commission. These two strategies caused widespread poverty and starvation among the farmers on the islands of Java and Sumatra. These were the same cruel methods that they had developed to force production of spices in the Spice Islands. So, although the farmers were not technically slaves, they had lost all freedom to manage their crops and their lives as they wished.

The VOC used the forced-delivery coffee system to monopolize production and set the price of coffee on the European market high, limiting the amount produced by burning trees down when necessary. (In 1650, the Dutch had burned down all the clove trees on all the Banda Islands but one, Ambon, and carried out a savage tree-cutting program just to keep prices up.) The Dutch government eventually set up a labor control system that maintained full command over the activity of the coffee producers. In 1785 the VOC ordered a switch in coffee cultivation from smallholder production to big estates that the company established. Twenty years later, the Dutch government systematically organized the farmers' labor on these large estates, transforming the system so they could totally manage the amount produced by the labor control system. There was no longer a need to destroy any trees—they simply disallowed farmers to produce coffee. It was much more convenient to destroy the lives of the farmers than to cut down trees that they might quickly put back into production.

In 1860 Eduard Douwes Dekker, a Dutchman who wrote under the pen name of Multatuli, wrote the novel *Max Havelaar: Or the Coffee Auctions of the Dutch Trading Company*—a protest work that played a critical role in developing a new policy in the colonial Dutch East Indies in the nineteenth and early twentieth centuries. The hero of the story, Max Havelaar, battles against the system of corrupt government in Indonesia. The book raised Europeans' awareness of the wealth and products they enjoyed as a result of the unethical

Javanese coffee market, 1802. (From T. S. Raffles, *The History of Java* [London: John Murray, 1830], p. 242.)

exploitation of people in the colonies. Eventually, this book influenced foreign policy of several colonial powers and was called "the book that killed colonialism."[1]

While the Dutch production of coffee in Java exemplified a situation where the growing, processing, marketing, and distribution of a commodity was under the complete control of a single corporation, the growth and development of the coffee industry in other parts of the world followed unpredictable forces of politics and burgeoning markets.

COFFEE IN BRAZIL

The Sons of Liberty dressed up as Narragansett Indians and, armed with small hatchets and clubs, made their way aboard the British merchant ships *Dartmouth*, *Beaver*, and *Eleanor*, which were moored in Boston Harbor. Swiftly and efficiently, all of the casks of tea were brought up from the hold to the deck, betraying the fact that at least some of the Indians were really longshoremen. The casks were opened and almost fifty tons of tea worth an estimated ten thousand pounds was unceremoniously dumped into the bay. Thus began America's long march toward becoming the world's premier consumer of coffee. To be pro-independence meant to be anti-British, and to drink anything but tea fit neatly into that definition.

Coffee drinking was a patriotic act while tea consumption was considered almost traitorous. Strangely, however, while coffee drinking was a sign of freedom and national sovereignty, it was also a sadly contradictory symbol. A new country, founded on the principles of freedom and democracy, chose coffee as a national beverage—a commodity that was wholly established on the blood and sweat of imported African slaves. No other commodity at this time perhaps other than sugar represented slavery to the same extent as coffee did; yet, it was coffee that was chosen as the country's national beverage.

Although coffee consumption was not very popular until the revolution, anti-British sentiment drove its increasing popularity. It was a quirk of history that the rise of European colonialism dictated where coffee was produced, while the end of colonialism resulted in its unparalleled consumption in America.

In retaliation to the United States, the British parliament banned coffee shipments from the Caribbean. Few countries, including Portuguese-ruled Brazil, volunteered to defy Britain and supply the United States. The one exception was France, Britain's traditional rival, whose Caribbean colonies, particularly Saint Domingue (Haiti) and the French Antilles, were capable of filling the gap.

It was not until 1808 when Napoleon marched into Lisbon, forcing the Portuguese prince to sail for Brazil, that America had broader access to coffee from the Latin American region.

Although Colonel Francisco de Melo Palheta's initial introduction of coffee to Brazil's northeast region of Para was not particularly successful because of the agro-climatic conditions, it was quickly discovered that the southeast region was ideally suited for coffee growth. The southeast had been originally exploited for gold and other precious metals, so the land itself had retained all its original fertility. As the metals ran out, coffee was introduced and the slave labor left over from the mining operations was immediately put to work growing and harvesting coffee.

It is difficult to imagine what a Brazilian coffee plantation was like in the early days. We can, however, put our imaginations to rest and read the descriptive work *Brazil and the Brazilians* by Kidder and Fletcher, published in 1857:

I cannot enter into the details of my journey in Minas-Geraes, but I am reluctant to pass over a visit to one of the finest plantations in the province. The proprietor was a Brazilian, and the whole fazenda, in its minutest details, was carried on in the manner peculiar to the country, without any admixture of foreign modes of government and culture.

Twelve miles beyond the Parahibuna (an affluent of the Parahiba) we turned aside from the highway, and, after riding through a belt of enclosed forest-land, we saw before us the large plantation house of Soldade, belonging to Senhor Commendador Silva Pinto.

The approach to the mansion was between two rows of palm-trees, around whose trunks a beautiful bignonia (the venusta) entwined itself, and then threw its climbing branches over the feathery leaves of the palms, thus forming a magnificent arch of flowers and foliage. The buildings, in the form of a hollow square, occupied an acre of ground. On two sides of the square was the residence of the Commendador and his family, while the remaining sides consisted of the sugar-establishment and the dwellings of the slaves. We entered the court-yard by a high gateway, and then for the first time we perceived the venerable planter sitting in a second-story veranda, reading. So soon as he saw us he laid down his book, descended into the square, and with great affability bade us a warm welcome. . . .

Servants flew about noiselessly at the commands of the Commendador: they gave us rooms, hot coffee, hot baths, &c. &c. Then both they and their master did that which is most grateful to the weary traveller: they let us alone.

When I had performed my ablutions and was recovered from fatigue, I went to the veranda where the Commendador had been reading. . . . I looked from the veranda upon a scene of cultivation. Close at hand were one hundred and fifty hives with bees; gently-rounded hills were covered with grazing flocks and herds, cotton and sugar fields were in valleys, while Indian corn and mandioca in large tracts were far to our right. The orange-orchard was the largest that I ever saw in any land: it was computed that there were ten thousand bushels of six different kinds of the luscious fruit. The sweet lemon abounded to such an extent that it was estimated that there were five thousand bushels. . . .

Of all the articles mentioned above, not one finds its way to market. They are for the sustenance and clothing of the slaves, of whom the Commendador formerly had seven hundred. These are engaged in cultivating coffee, (for this is the great coffee region,) which is the only crop intended by the proprietor to bring back a pecuniary return. This senhor owns other plantations, but that of Soldade contains an area of sixty-four square miles.

At dinner we were served in a large dining-room. The Commendador sat at the head of the table, while his guests and the various free members of his family sat upon forms, the feitors (overseers) and shepherds being at the lower end. He lives in true baronial style. . . . A pleasant conversation was kept up during the long repast, and at its close three servants came, one bearing a massive silver bowl a foot and a half in diameter, another a pitcher of the same material containing warm water, while a third carried towels. The newly-arrived guests were thus served in lieu of finger-basins, which are rarely seen outside the capital. . . .

In the course of our conversation the Commendador told us that he had his "own music now." He spoke of it very humbly. We desired to hear his musicians, supposing that we should hear a wheezy plantation-fiddle, a fife, and a drum. The Commendador said that we should be gratified. An hour after vespers

I heard the twanging of violins, the tuning of flutes, short voluntaries on sundry bugles, the clattering of trombones, and all those musical symptoms preparatory to a beginning of some march, waltz, or polka. I went to the room whence proceeded these sounds; there I beheld fifteen slave musicians, a regular band. I was totally unprepared for this. But the next piece overwhelmed me with surprise: the choir, accompanied by the instruments, performed a Latin mass.[2]

Unfortunately, this idyllic scene belied the true nature of Brazilian coffee faziendas. Slaves were chattel and treated no better than the furniture. Earlier in the same book by Kidder and Fletcher, the authors state:

Until 1850, when the slave-trade was effectually put down, it was considered cheaper, on the country-plantations, to use up a slave in five or seven years and purchase another, than to take care of him. This I had, in the interior, from intelligent native Brazilians, and my own observation has confirmed it.[3]

Slaves were forced to work sixteen to eighteen hours a day, keep their ramshackle residences clean, take care of their personal needs, and entertain the plantation owner as requested. Slaves were regarded as being less than human. Because of the enormous success and growth of the coffee industry, Brazil maintained slavery for longer than any other Western country. Even after slavery was declared illegal in Brazil in 1888, plantation owners continued to fight against abolition, fearing it would bring an end to the country's coffee industry—and their own wealth.

Employing a combination of vast fertile lands and cheap slave labor, Brazil quickly became a major producer of coffee. This caused coffee prices to drop, further expanding the market, particularly in the United States. New Brazilian varieties of arabica coffee were developed along with the distribution networks to move coffee to the ports of export.

By 1850 Brazil was producing more than half the world's coffee. Even though slave labor was abolished in

Work on a Brazilian fazienda. (From H. C. Dent, *A Year in Brazil* [London: Trench and Company, 1886], p. 52.)

the latter part of the nineteenth century, the Brazilians made up for this loss of cheap labor through the rapacious exploitation of their land resources. They destroyed the rain forests at an unprecedented rate and replaced them with coffee. As the land lost its fertility, ever more land was usurped for coffee production.

The low cost of coffee coming from Brazil turned America into a land of coffee drinkers. Coffee became so important to the American diet that it was considered to be a strategic necessity during both world wars. The ubiquitous "cup of Joe" reflected the GIs' need for coffee in their daily rations.

FAIR TRADE COFFEE

At the close of the Second World War, under the umbrella of the newly formed United Nations, a major effort was launched to ensure stable control and trade of international commodities under the Havana Charter (1948). In the early part of the 1950s, there was a major decline in the price of most primary commodities, including coffee and cocoa. Shortly thereafter, the Fair Trade movement— begun as alternative trade organizations—emerged in Europe and the United States to promote grassroots development through direct and equitable trade. These organizations bought their goods directly from developing country producers and paid them a fair price while providing technical assistance and developing market contacts. These organizations had limited but useful success in raising producer incomes and exposing products to new markets. They initially dealt mainly in handicrafts, and today there are more than three thousand of these shops in Europe called the Network of European World Shops, and about one hundred are in the United States, all organized under the Fair Trade Federation and all selling goods from developing countries without the need for middlemen.

In 1962 an international agreement on coffee was reached while the United Nations provided the diplomatic umbrella under which representatives from developing countries were able to meet and refine proposals to improve their trade positions. Among the UN bodies that sought to promote the training interests of developing countries was the United Nations Conference on Trade and Development (UNCTAD), established in Geneva in 1964. With a heavy representation of developing countries, UNCTAD supported the greater transfer of wealth from the North to the South through economic aid, and more important, more equitable trade conditions. This new fair trade initiative was based on two key provisions: (1) the removal of the inequitable protectionist regulations of importing countries, and (2) the creation of some form of interventionist mechanisms to guarantee "fair" prices for the agricultural commodities produced in the South. Unfortunately, the rich importing countries felt that this scheme would pose too great a threat on their far-flung interests and convinced other members of UNCTAD to vote against all resolutions. The UNCTAD initiative failed.

With the failure of the United Nations to establish fair trade, the initiative was passed on to the private sector. In 1959 a group of young people from the Catholic political party in the Dutch town of Kerkrade formed the *Fair Trade Organizatie*. Although it started off with the goal of training, it soon switched strategies and began purchasing products from developing countries for sale in the Netherlands. In 1969 the first shop to sell sugar through better prices to farmers in developing countries was opened in the Netherlands.

In order to promote the concept of spending a little extra to purchase fair trade products, the fair trade network in Holland established the Max Havelaar fair trade labeling initiative in 1988. The goal was to obtain higher prices for commodities produced by poor farmers in developing countries in order to break the cycle of poverty they were locked into.

The fair trade movement encountered severe competition when it came to coffee simply because there was a global oversupply of this commodity as a result of increased production in traditional coffee-producing countries. It was greatly exacerbated by the entrance of newcomers into the coffee sector, especially Vietnam, which started with an extremely small base and ended up being the world's second-largest producer by the close of the twentieth century. A good deal of responsibility for this disaster rests with the World Bank and the International Monetary Fund, which encouraged, indeed almost forced, developing countries to increase commodity exports in order to earn foreign exchange to meet their debt payments. The World Bank policies unfortunately reflected the old saying that the road to hell was paved with good intentions.

More recently, socially minded consumers are starting to understand and agree with the notion that producers in developing countries should be paid a fair price for their labor and their goods. Fair trade coffee sales have grown rapidly and products can be found in a great many supermarkets. Often, because they are produced in smallholder operations and subjected to greater hands-on control, fair trade commodities are generally superior in quality, but there is no guarantee of this. Because the profile of coffee consumption in the United States has changed so dramatically in the last decade, the greatest opportunity for fair trade coffee rests with the coffeehouse chains. Some of them currently purchase fair trade coffee—such as Starbucks—and no doubt will increase their commitments to these products since they hold such a powerful promotional pull for consumers. From their end, fair trade producers must understand the critical need of operations, such as the coffeehouse chains, for the strictest possible adherence to consistent, high quality.

In order to be fair trade certified, the products have to follow specific principles and practices in production and trading relationships. For those readers who are interested in fair trade products, here are the basic principles behind them:

Products should create opportunities for smaller producers so that the fair trade practice expresses a strategy for poverty alleviation and sustainable development. They must create opportunities for producers who have been disadvantaged or marginalized by the conventional trading system.

Fair trade operations must have transparent management systems and always deal equitably with trading partners.

Fair trade is a means to develop producers' independence. Fair trade relationships provide continuity, during which producers and their marketing organizations can improve their management skills and their access to new markets.

A fair price in the regional or local context is one that has been agreed through dialogue and participation. It covers not only the costs of production but enables production which is socially just and environmentally sound. It provides fair pay to the producers and takes into account the principle of equal pay for equal work by women and men.

Fair traders ensure prompt payment to their partners and, whenever possible, help producers with access to pre-harvest or pre-production financing.

They also provide money for free primary schools and health care, which really help the people who are not earning enough to send their children to school.

Fair trade means that the work of men and women is properly valued and rewarded. Each person is always paid for their contribution to the production process and is empowered in their organizations, regardless of gender.

Fair trade means a safe and healthy working environment for producers. The participation of children (if any) does not adversely affect their well-being, security, educational requirements and need for play and conforms to the UN Convention on the Rights of the Child as well as the law and norms in the local context.

Fair trade actively encourages better environmental practices and the application of responsible methods of production. Fair trade certifiers for example strictly prohibit the use of genetically modified organisms (GMOs) and promote integrated farm management systems that improve soil fertility as well as preserving valuable ecosystems for future generations.[4]

As time progresses and pressures mount in consuming countries to observe more and more ethical production methods for coffee, it is hoped that unfair prices for producers, unfit working conditions for laborers, and abusive employment of children will become practices of the past and nothing more than a footnote in coffee's dark history.

PART 2

Coffee's Place in Culture and Economic Development

7

Early Coffeehouse Culture

Coffeehouses, regardless of their location, had the effect of bringing people together in an animated discourse. Because of caffeine's ability to keep drinkers awake and mentally sharp, the discussions would often revolve around intellectual subjects: politics, the arts, science, and economics. Because of this, in countries ruled by monarchies or dictators, coffeehouses always came under the state's scrutiny because of the fear that group gatherings might generate new, revolutionary ideas that could threaten the state's stability or existence.

Elegant surroundings, intellectually stimulating entertainment such as the reading of prose and poetry, and an aura of refinement marked the development of coffeehouses around the world. Often, in each country, they would represent the epitome of architecture, style, and taste. The patrons of any establishment had a tendency to be loyal to that particular establishment and met with other patrons of similar mind, interests, and taste. Businessmen met with other businessmen and academics met with other academics. It did not take long before like-minded people formed groups or societies, some of which became venerable institutions and have lasted to the present day, such as the Royal Society or Lloyds of London.

Great coffeehouses of the Middle East became centers for carpet or spice traders. Astronomers may have congregated in a particular coffeehouse in Alexandria; cart drivers may have had their favorite spot in the Bosporus port of Constantinople; silk carpet dealers sat down in the silk markets of Bursa, and caravan operators had their coffee klatch in the heart of the Khartoum souk.

Thus, coffeehouses served as natural centers of gravity where people could congregate and join in the lively discussion of subjects that were dear to them. These gathering places served not only the immediate needs of their patrons but would eventually serve as the home base of some of the world's greatest institutions.

Nowhere was this more apparent than in England, particularly during the post-Reformation period. It is a time that can legitimately be called the Golden Age of Coffee.

It is difficult to determine just why coffeehouses became so popular in England. Perhaps it was a Republican reaction to the inequities of the English class system. It is important to understand that a primary concern of coffeehouse keepers was that their establishments be opened to patrons of all classes. In a sense, this made coffeehouses a social movement. Because certain members of the lower class could be rather boisterous, certain rules were to be adhered to ensure that no patrons would feel intimidated. Just to give an example of the liberal traditions that coffeehouses engendered, look at the following sets of regulations displayed on the walls of several seventeenth-century coffeehouses. Written in the form of a poem, it gives an idea of what coffeehouse behavior was expected to be.

The Rules and Orders of the Coffeehouse

Enter, Sirs, freely, but first, if you please,
Peruse our civil orders, which are these.
First, gentry, tradesmen, are all welcome hither,
And may without affront sit down together;
Pre-eminence of place none here should mind,
But take the next fit seat that he can find;
Nor need any, if finer persons come,
Rise up to assign to them his room;
To limit men's expense, we think not fair,
But let him forfeit twelve-pence that shall swear;
He that shall any quarrel here begin,
Shall give each man a dish t'atone the sin;
And so shall he, whose compliments extend

So far to drink in coffee to his friend;
Let noise of loud disputes be quiet forborne,
No maudlin lovers here in corners mourn,
But all be brisk and talk, but not too much,
On sacred things, let none presume to touch.
Nor profane Scripture, nor sawcily wrong
Affairs of state with an irreverent tongue;
Left mirth be innocent, and each man see
That all his jests without reflection be;
To keep the house more quiet and from blame,
We banish hence cards, dice, and every game;
Nor can allow of wagers, that exceed
Five shillings, which ofttimes much trouble breed;
Let all that's lost or forfeited be spent
In such good liquor and the house doth vent.
And customers endeavor, to their powers,
For to observe still, seasonable hours.
Lastly, let each man what he calls for pay,
And so you're welcome to come every day.

As noted earlier, the first coffeehouse in England was opened in the university town of Oxford in the year 1650 by a Lebanese Jew by the name of Jacob. Thus began the great coffee movement that would eventually take over all of England. The next establishment to open was the Oxford Coffee Club in 1655. Because of the congenial atmosphere and animated conversation, the greatest scientists of Oxford University became regular patrons, along with their students. Great theories and the results of the most recent experiments and calculations were the subjects of enthusiastic discussion. The central group included such men as Sir Robert Boyle (chemist), John Wilkins (clergyman and author—the only person to have headed a college at both Oxford and Cambridge universities), John Evelyn (author of several books on gardening, conservation of forests, and navigation), Robert Hooke (one of Britain's greatest scientists and considered by some to be Leonardo da Vinci's equal), Christopher Wren (architect of St. Paul's Cathedral and the royal astronomer), and William Petty (at the time England's most famous economist and philosopher). They became the core of the world's most prestigious scientific league—the Royal Society. The group eventually moved to London and was officially established on November 28, 1660, when twelve of the coffeehouse patrons met at Gresham College and attended an opening lecture by Christopher Wren, who was then the Gresham professor of astronomy. The list of presidents, officers, and members of the Royal Society over the years constitutes a veritable who's who in the history of science. No other scientific organization in history can closely compare to the Royal Society and its accomplishments over the years.

London's first official coffeehouse was opened in 1652 by Pasqua Rosée in St. Michael's Alley, Cornhill, London. A native of Turkey, Rosée not only knew how to brew coffee but was also very effective in promoting it. He wrote and printed the first handbill advertising the benefits of coffee, which at the time was a new and remarkable social innovation. A copy of this advertisement is in the British Museum and is reprinted here:

The Vertue Of The COFFEE Drink,

First made and publicly sold in England
by Pasqua Rosee

The grain or berry called coffee, groweth upon little Trees, only in the Deserts of Arabia. It is brought from thence, and drunk generally throughout all the Grand Seigniors Dominions.

It is a simple innocent thing, composed into a Drink, by being dryed in an Oven and ground to Powder, and boiled up with Spring water, and about half a pint of it to be drunk, fasting an hour before, and not Eating an hour after, and to be taken as hot as possibly can be endured; the which will never fetch the skin off the mouth, or raise any Blisters, by reason of that Heat.

The Turks drink at meals and other times, is usually Water, and there Dyet consists much of Fruit & the Crudites whereof are very much corrected by this Drink.

The quality of this Drink is cold and Dry; and though it be a Dryer; yet it neither heats, nor inflames more than hot Posset.

It so closeth the Orifice of the Stomack, and fortifies the heat within, that it's very good to help digestion; and therefore of great use to be drunk about 3 or 4 a Clock in the afternoon, as well as in the morning.

It quickens the Spirits and makes the Heart Lightsome. It is good against sore eys, and the better if you hold your Head o'er it, and take in the Steem that way.

It suppresseth Fumes exceedingly, and therefore good against the Head-ach, and will very much stop the Defluxion of Rhuems, that distil from the Head upon the Stomack, and so prevent and help Consumption and the Cough of the Lungs.

It is excellent to prevent and cure the Dropsy, Gout and Scurvy.

It is known by experience to be better than any other Drying Drink for People in years, or Children that have any running humors up on them, as the Kings Evil. Etc.

It is very good to prevent Mis-carryings in Child-bearing Women.

It is a most excellent Remedy against the Spleen, Hypocondriack Winds, or the like.

It will prevent Drowsiness, and make one fit for business, if one have occasion to Watch; and therefore you are not to Drink of it after Supper, unless you intend to be watchful, for it will hinder sleep for 3 or 4 hours.

It is believed that in Turkey, where this is generally drunk, that they are not troubled with the Stone, Gout, Dropsie, or Scurvy, and that their Skins are exceeding clear and white.

It is neither Laxative nor Restringent.

> Made and Sold in St. Michaels Alley,
> in Cornhill by Pasqua Rosee,
> at the Signe of his own Head

However, not everyone agreed that coffee was all that these claims made it out to be. The poem "A Cup of Coffee, or Coffee in Its Colours," published in 1663, was rather critical of the brew:

> For men and Christians to turn Turks and think
> To excuse the crime, because 'tis in their drink!
> Pure English apes! ye might, for aught I know,
> Would it but mode learn to eat spiders too.
> Should any of your grandsires' ghosts appear
> In your wax-candle circles, and but hear
> The name of coffee so much called upon,
> Then see it drank like scalding Phlegethon;
> Would they not startle, think ye, all agreed
> 'Twas conjuration both in word and deed?[1]

Pasqua Rosée eventually left the country, and his establishment fell into the hands of his English partner. London's second coffeehouse proprietor, James Farr, did not achieve the same personal fame as Rosée, but his establishment, the Rainbow, which opened on Fleet Street in 1657, did become very well known in London. One of its patrons was Sir Henry Blount, author of the famous book *A Voyage into the Levant*. Naturally, anybody wanting to know anything about coffee would go to the Rainbow and get the information directly from the man who had been throughout the region where coffee was originally established. In fact, Sir Henry Blount is occasionally referred to as "the father of English coffeehouses."[2]

Coffee received a boost as a result of the first newspaper advertisement devoted specifically to the beverage. On May 26, 1657, the weekly pamphlet the *Publick Adviser* contained the following ad:

> In Bartholomew Lane on the back side of the Old Exchange, the drink called Coffee, (which is a very wholsom and Physical drink, having many excellent vertues, closes the Orifice of the Stomack, fortifies the heat within, helpeth Digestion, quicketh the Spirits, maketh the heart lightsom, is good against Eye-sores, Coughs or Colds, Rhumes, Consumptions, Head-ach, Dropsie, Gout, Scurvy, Kings Evil, and many others is to be sold both in the morning, and at three of the clock in the afternoon.

London's Rota Coffee Club, which met at Miles coffeehouse, was founded in 1659 as a political club. Rota referred to the rotation of members of Parliament. It was actually a debate club and it attracted some of England's most astute political commentators. Among the Rota's most renowned patrons was John Milton.

Milton (1608–1674) is considered to be one of the greatest poets of the English language. Although he is best known for his epic poem *Paradise Lost*, he also dedicated himself to penning a considerable amount of prose on both history and politics. Milton was a charter member of the Rota Coffee Club. In 1660 he wrote *The Ready and Easy Way to Establish a Free Commonwealth*. In a 1915 edition of this book, the notes describe the Rota Club thusly:

> Among the various contemporary schools of commonwealth-proposers there was none so interesting, so brilliant, and so important in relation to Milton as the little group of enthusiasts who met regularly during the winter evenings of 1659–60 to discuss 'aierie modells' under the hospitable shelter of Miles' Coffee-House, 'at the Turk's head, in the New Pallace-yard.' The founder and animating spirit of this famous debating society was James Harrington, the author of *Oceana*, and, upon the whole, the ablest political philosopher of his time. Toland styles him the 'greatest Commonwealthman in the World,' and his *Oceana* 'the most perfect Form of Popular Government that ever was.' The *Oceana* appeared in 1656. It was instantly pounced upon by Cromwell's courtiers, and carried to Whitehall; but, through Harrington's intercession with Lady Claypole, the 'child of his brain' was rescued from Cromwell. Toland tells us that the treatise was 'greedily bought up, and become the subject of all mens discourse.' It proposed a most elaborate model of a commonwealth, based upon rotation in office, equal distribution of land, and the fundamental principle 'that empire follows the balance of property, whether lodg'd in one, in a few, or

in many hands'—a principle which, Toland affirms, Harrington 'was the first that ever made out.' Aubrey records that this 'ingeniose tractat, together with . . . smart discourses and inculcations, dayly at coffee-houses, made many proselytes.' It provoked spirited controversy, and became the political creed and unifying principle of the Rota Club.[3]

Clearly, England at the time wasn't the most convenient place to debate opposing political positions. Samuel Pepys records the following notation in his diary on January 10, 1660:

> James Harrington, the political writer, author of "Oceana," and founder of a club called The Rota, in 1659, which met at Miles's coffee-house in Old Palace Yard, and lasted only a few months. In 1661 he was sent to the Tower, on suspicion of treasonable designs. His intellects appear to have failed afterwards, and he died 1677.[4]

Yet, in 1665, one of London's pamphleteers wrote that "Coffee and Commonwealth came in together for a Reformation to make's a free and sober nation . . . where men of differing judgments crowd." Adding to that, the coffeehouse was where men could discourse freely.

But the coffeehouses—as well as all of London—faced some formidable challenges. The Great Fire of London took place in 1666. The conflagration swept through the central part of the city from Sunday, September 2 to Wednesday, September 5, completely destroying the medieval section of the city bound by the original Roman walls. The fire destroyed more than thirteen thousand houses and untold numbers of businesses. After the fire, a great many new coffeehouses opened in much finer quarters than their predecessors. Coffee became so popular that men were spending more time in the coffeehouse than at home. This situation precipitated the famous *Women's Petition against Coffee*, published in 1674. Written by an anonymous "Well-willer," the pamphlet was in reality a satire directed against the political authorities. It is a brilliant work that is quoted here:

The Women's Petition against Coffee

Representing to Publick Consideration the Grand Inconveniencies accruing to their Sex from the Excessive Use of that drying, Enfeebling Liquor.

Presented to the Right Honorable the Keepers of the Liberty of Venus.

By a Well-willer

London, Printed 1674.

To the Right Honorable the Keepers of the Liberties of Venus; The Worshipful Court of Female Assistants, &c.

The Humble Petitions and Address of Several Thousands of Buxome Good-Women, Languishing in Extremity of Want.

Sheweth,

this stuff That since 'tis Reckon'd amongst the
Glories of our Native Country, To be a Paradise for
Women: The fame in our Apprehensions can consist
in nothing more than the brisk Activity of our men,
who in former Ages were justly esteemed the Ablest
Performers in Christendome; But to our unspeakable
Grief, we find of late a very sensible Decay of that true
Old English Vigor; our Gallants being every way so
Frenchified, that they are become meer Cock-
sparrows, fluttering things that come on Sa sa, with a
world of Fury, but are not able to stand to it, and in
the very first Charge fall down flat before us. Never
did Men wear greater breeches, or carry less in them
of any Mettle whatsoever. There was a glorious Dis-
pensation ('twas surely in the Golden Age) when
Lusty Ladds of Seven or eigh hundred years old, Got
Sons and Daughters; ande we have read, how a Prince
of Spain was forced to make a Law, that Men should
not Repeat the Grand Kindness to their Wives, above
NINE times a night; but Alas! Alas! Those forwards
Days are gone, The dull Lubbers want a Spur now,
rather than a Bridle: being so far from dowing any
works of Supererregation that we find them not
capable of performing those Devoirs which their
Duty, and our Expectations Exact.

The Occasion of which Insufferable Disaster,
after a furious Enquiry, and Discussion of the Point by
the Learned of the Faculty, we can Attribute to
nothing more than the Excessive use of that Newfan-
gled, Abominable, Heathenish Liquor called

COFFEE, which Riffling Nature of her Choicest Treasures, and Drying up the Radical Moisture, has so Eunucht our Husbands, and Cripple our more kind Gallants, that they are become as Impotent as Age, and as unfruitful as those Desarts whence that unhappy Berry is said to be brought.

For the continual flipping of this pitiful drink is enough to bewitch Men of two and twenty, and tie up the Codpiece-points without a Charm. It renders them that us it as Lean as Famine, as Rivvel'd as Envy, or an old meager Hagg over-ridden by an Incubus. They come from it with nothing moist but their snotty Noses, nothing stiffe but their Joints, nor standing but their Ears: They pretend 'twill keep them Waking, but we find by scurvy Experience, they sleep quietly enough after it. A Betrothed Queen might trust her self a bed with one of them, without the nice Caution of a sword between them: nor can call all the Art we use revive them from this Lethargy, so unfit they are for Action, that like young Train-band-men when called upon Duty, their Ammunition is wanting; peradventure they Present, but cannot give Fire, or at least do but flash in the Pan, instead of doing execution.

Nor let any Doating, Superstitious Catos shake their Goatish Beards, and task us of Immodesty for this Declaration, since 'tis a publick Grievance, and cries abound for Reformation. Weight and Measure, 'tis well known, should go throughout the world, and there is no torment like Famishment. Experience witnesses our Damage, and Necessity (which easily supersedes all the Laws of Decency) justifies our com-

plaints: For can any Woman of Sense or Spirit endure
with Patience, that when priviledg'd by Legal Ceremonies, she approaches the Nuptial Bed, expecting a
Man that with Sprightly Embraces, should Answer
the Vigour of her Flames, she on the contrary should
only meat A Bedful of Bones, and hug a meager useless Corpse rendred as sapless as a Kixe, and dryer
than a Pumice-Stone, by the perpetual Fumes of
Tobacco, and bewitching effects of this most perni-
tious COFFEE, where by Nature is Enfeebled, the
Off-spring of our Mighty Ancestors Dwindled into a
Succession of Apes and Pigmies: and

—The Age of Man

Now Cramp't into an Inch, that was a Span.

Nor is this (though more than enough!) All the
ground of our Complaint: For besides, we have
reason to apprehend and grow Jealous, That Men by
frequenting these Stygian Tap-houses will usurp on
our Prerogative of tattling, and soon learn to exceed
us in Talkativeness: a Quality wherein our Sex has
ever Claimed preheminence: For here like so many
Frogs in a puddle, they sup muddy water, and
murmur insignificant notes till half a dozen of them
out-babble an equal number of us at a Gossipping,
talking all at once in Confusion, and running from
point to point as insensibly, and swiftly, as ever the
Ingenous Pole-wheel could run divisions on the Base-
viol; yet in all their prattle every one abounds in his
own sense, as stiffly as a Quaker at the late Barbican
Dispute, and submits to the Reasons of no othre
mortal: so that there being neither Moderator nor

Rules observ'd, you mas as soon fill a Quart pot with Syllogismes, as profit by their Discourses. . . .

So once more they troop to the Sack-shop till they are drunker than before; and then by a retrograde motion, stagger back to Soberize themselves with Coffee: thus like Tennis Balls between two Rackets, the Fopps our Husbands are bandied to and fro all day between the Coffee-house and Tavern, whilst we poor souls sit mopeing all alone till Twelve at night, and when at last they come to bed finoakt like a Westphalia Hogs-head we have no more comfort of them, than from a shotten Herring or a dried Bulrush; which forces us to take up this Lamentation and sing,

> Tom Farthing, Tom Farthing, where has
>   thou been, Tom Farthing?
> Twelve a Clock e're you come in, Two a
>   clock ere you begin, And
> then at last can do nothing: Would make a
>   Woman weary, weary,
> weary, would make a Woman weary, &c.

Wherefore the Premises considered, and to the end that our Just Rights may be restored, and all the Ancient Priviledges of our Sex preserved inviolable; That our Husbands may give us some other Testimonial of their being Men, besides their Beards and wearing of empty Pantaloons: That they no more run the hazard of being Cuckol'd by Dildo's: But returning to the good old strengthening Liquors of our Forefathers; that Natures Exchequer may once again be replenisht, and a Race of

Lusty Hero's begot, able by their Atchievements, to equal the Glories of our Ancestors.

We Humbly Pray, That you our Trusty Patrons would improve your Interest, that henceforth the Drinking COFFEE may on severe penalties be forbidden to all Persons under the Age of Threescore; and that instead thereof, Lusty nappy Beer, Cock-Ale, Cordial Canaries, Restoring Malago's, and Back-recruiting Chochole be Recommended to General Use, throughout the Utopian Territories.

> In hopes of which Glorious Reformation,
>   your Petitioners shall readily Prostrate
>   themselves, and ever Pray, &c.
> FINIS.

This brilliant piece of satire could not go unanswered, and later in the same year the *Men's Answer to the Women's Petition against Coffee* was published:

THE
Mens Answer
TO THE
Womens Petition
AGAINST
COFFEE,
VINDICATING

Their own Performances, and the Vertues of that Liquor, from the Undeserved Aspersions lately cast upon them by their

SCANDALOUS PAMPHLET.
LONDON:
Printed in the Year 1674.
Could it be Imagined, that ungrateful Women, after so much laborious Drudgery, both by Day and Night, and the best of our Blood and Spirits spent in your Service, you should thus publickly Complain? Certain we are, that there never was Age or Nation more Indulgent to your Sex; have we not condiscended to all the Methods of Debauchery?

Invented more Postures than *Aretine* ever Dreamed of! Been Pimps to our own Wives, and Courted Gallants even with the hazard of our Estates, to do us the Civility of making us not only Contented, but most obliged Cuckolds: Is he thought worthy to be esteemed a Gentleman, that has not seaven times pass'd the Torrid Zone of a Venerial Distemper, or does not maintain, at least, a Brace of Mistresses; Talk not to us of those Doating Fumblers of seven or eight hundred years Old, a Larke is better than a Kite; and Cock-Sparrows, though not long liv'd, are undoubtedly preferrable for the work of Generation before dull Ravens, though some think they live three hundred years: That our Island is a Paradise for Women, is verified still by the brisk Activity of our Men, who with an equal Contempt scorn *Italian* Padlocks, and defie *French* Dildo's, knowing that a small Doze of Natures Quintessence, satisfies better in a Female Limbeck, than the largest Potion infused by Art. . . .

But why must innocent COFFEE be the object of your Spleen? That harmless and healing Liquor,

which Indulgent Providence first sent amongst us, at a
time when Brimmers of Rebellion, and Fanatick Zeal
had intoxicated the Nation, and we wanted a Drink
at once to make us Sober and Merry: 'Tis not this
incomparable settle Brain that shortens Natures Standard, or makes us less Active in the Sports of *Venus*,
and we wonder you should take these Exceptions,
since so many of the little Houses, with the Turkish
Woman stradling on their Signs, are but Emblems of
what is to be done within for your Conveniencies,
meer Nurseries to promote the petulant Trade, and
breed up a stock of hopeful Plants for the future service of the Republique, in the most thriving Mysteries
of Debauchery; There being scarce a Coffee-Hut but
affords a Tawdry Woman, a wonton Daughter, or a
Buxome Maide, to accommodate Customers; and can
you think that any which frequent such Discipline,
can be wanting in their Pastures, or defective in their
Arms? The News we Chat of there, you will not think
it Impertinent, when you consider the fair opportunities you have thereby, of entertaining an obliging
friend in our Absence, and how many of us you have
dubb'd Knights of the Bull-Feather, whilst we have
sate innocently sipping the Devils Holy-water; we do
not call it so for driving the Cace-dæmon of Letchery
out of us, for the truth is, it rather assists us for your
Nocturnal Benevolencies, by drying up those Crude
Flatulent Humours, which otherwise would make us
only Flash in the Pan, without doing that Thundering
Execution which your Expectations Exact, we dare
Appeal to Experience in the Case.

Coffee is the general Drink throughout Turky, and those *Eastern* Regions, and yet no part of the world can boast more able or eager performers, than those Circumcised Gentlemen, who, (like our modern Gallants) own no other joys of Heaven, than what consists in Veneral Titillations; the Physical qualities of this Liquor are almost Innumerable and its vertues (if you will beleive *Pointing*, able to out-noise the Quackbil of an all-healing Doctor, when your kindness at the Close Hugg has bestowed on us a virulent Gonorrhæa, this is our Catholicon, *Ens Naturæ* and *Aqua Tetrachymagogon* is an Ass to it, 'Tis base adulterate wine and surcharges of Muddy Ale that enfeeble nature, makes a man as salatious as a Goat, and yet as impotent as Age, whereas Coffee Collects and settles the Spirits, makes the erection more Vigorous, the Ejaculation more full, adds a spiritualescency to the Sperme, and renders it more firm and suitable to the Gusto of the womb, and proportionate to the ardours and expectation too, of the female Paramour. . . .

Cease then for the Future your Clamours against our civil Follies. Alas! alas! Dear Hearts, the Coffee house is the Citizens Academy, where he learns more Wit than ever his Grannum taught him, the Young-Gallants Stage where he displays the Wardrobe of his excellent no parts; 'Tis the Non Cons Bull-baiting, the News-mongers Exchange, the Fools business, the Knaves Ambuscade, and the Wise mans Recreation:

Here it is where we have the sparkling Cyder, the mighty Mum, and the back recruiting Chocolate; 'Tis Coffee that both keeps us Sober, or can make us so;

And let our Wives that hereafter shall presume to Petition against it, be confined to lie alone all Night, and
in the Day time drink nothing but Bonny Clabber.
    FINIS.

Among leading coffeehouses that survived the Great Fire
of London was the well-known Rainbow owned by
James Farr. In memory of his establishment's narrow
escape, he issued one of the first coffeehouse tokens.
Stamped with an arched rainbow rising from the bil-
lowing smoke of the fire, Farr's token was designed to
signify that all was well at the Rainbow coffeehouse. On
the opposite side of the coin was inscribed, "In Fleet
Street—His Half Penny."

Within a short period of time a great number of
these coffeehouse tokens were produced out of pewter,
brass, copper, and even gilded leather. They were
readily redeemed at face value in the coffeehouse they
represented.

As can be seen, it was common for tokens to display
the sign of the hand pouring coffee from an old Turkish
pot. The visages of Ottoman sultans Murat and
Suleiman were also common on these tokens. In 1674, a
royal proclamation called for the prosecution of anyone
privately producing coins or tokens, thus ending the
charming practice.

Because coffeehouses were taking business and
attention away from the alehouses, a steady stream of
propaganda against coffee started to grow. It often took

Richard Lione
in the Strand

Henry Muscut
opposite Brook House in Holborn

Mary Stringar
in Little Trinity Lane

West Country Coffee House
in Lothebury

Richard Tart
in Gray Friars, Newgate Street

Thomas Outridge
in Carter Lane End, near Creed Lane

William Russell
in St. Bartholomew's Close, Smithfield

Ward's Coffee House
in Bread Street

John Marston
in Trumpington Street, Cambridge

Mansfield's Coffee House
in Shoe Lane

English coffee tokens. (Print from William H. Ukers,
All about Coffee [New York: Tea and Coffee Trade
Journal Company, 1922].)

the form of pamphlets deriding the "character of a coffeehouse." One of the most effective attacks on coffee was a satire published in 1665 titled simply *The Character of a Coffee-House*. A few of its verses follow:

The Character of a Coffee-House

A Coffee-House, the learned hold
It is a place where Coffee's sold:
This derivation cannot fail us,
For where Ale's vended, that's an Ale-house.
This been granted to be true,
'Tis meet that next the Signs we shew
Both where and how to find this house
Where men such cordial broth carowse.

Look, there is a man who takes the steem
In at his Nose, as an extreme
Worm in his pate, and giddiness,
Ask him and he will say no less.
There sitteth one whose Droptick belly
Was hard as flint, now's soft as jelly.

The gallant he for Tea doth call,
The Usurer for naught at all.
The Pragmatick he doth intreat
That they will fill him some Beau-cheat,
The Virtuoso he cries hand me
Some Coffee mixt with Sugar-can be.

And so on and so on.

Of course, there were several pamphlets issued defending coffee and coffeehouses. One of the last to be issued before Charles II tried to curb the consumption of coffee was an eight-page work titled "Coffeehouses Vindicated," which described all the advantages of a coffeehouse over an alehouse.

Because he thought that coffeehouses were "seminaries of sedition," Charles II tried to suppress them in 1672 by asking the lord keeper and judges to provide him an opinion of how far he might go in legally prosecuting them. They provided him an answer so equivocal that he put off doing anything for three years. However, on December 23, 1675, the king issued a blunt proclamation whose purpose was "the suppression of coffeehouses." There was such discontent voiced among the vendors of coffee, tea, and chocolate that the proclamation was recalled.

The coffeehouses of the period were often referred to as "penny universities" because there was so much intellectual conversation going on within their walls.

> So great a Universitie
> I think there ne're was any:
> In which you may a Schoolar be
> For spending of a Penny

The waiters and waitresses who quickly brought the coffee were awarded by customers dropping coins into a box on the bar labeled, "To Insure Promptness." Hence began the practice of awarding a tip for service.

Soon the administrators of the British East India Company began agitating for greater consumption of tea because they had far more interests in that particular commodity than in coffee, which was largely the enterprise of the French and the Dutch. From as many as three thousand in London alone, the number of coffeehouses began to dwindle dramatically as tea took over. By the turn of the nineteenth century, coffeehouses had all but disappeared and tea became the entrenched English habit. Nonetheless, several famous coffeehouses continued to thrive.

Among the most famous of London's coffeehouses was Garraway's, located in the Cornhill district. It became a haven for mercantile transactions. Slaughter's coffeehouse in St. Martin's Lane attracted painters and sculptors. Among its patrons were Thomas Gainsborough, one of London's most illustrious portrait painters, and Giovanni Battista Cipriani, known for his engravings and decorations in Somerset House. Tom's coffeehouse in Birchin Lane became famous because of its association with David Garrick, the celebrated English actor, playwright, and manager of the Garrick Theatre. Another well-known coffeehouse was Lloyd's on Tower Street, which, because of its location, attracted many patrons who were involved in the shipping and marine insurance business. It eventually became Lloyd's of London, the world's largest insurer. Another notable spot was the Grecian, which became the home of Joseph

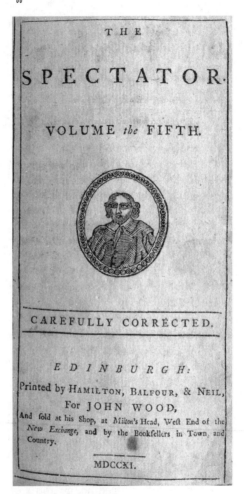

The *Spectator*, 1711.

Addison and Sir Richard Steele, the writers and publishers of the *Tatler* and the *Spectator*, Britain's most famous tabloids.

Italy's first coffeehouses did not serve nearly as important a function as those in England. Coffee was introduced to consumers long before coffeehouses were established by way of the *aquacedrataji*. These itinerant drink vendors wandered the cobblestoned Italian city streets, heartily calling out the beverages they dispensed such as lemonade, chocolate, and alcoholic liqueurs. As soon as coffee was introduced into Italy, the *aquacedrataji* added it to their menus and started to dispense it. The demand for coffee grew to a point that justified investment into a fixed establishment. Based upon the elegant Oriental coffeehouses of Constantinople, the first Italian coffeehouses were known as caffès, possibly from the name Kaffa, the region in Ethiopia where coffee originally came from. (To this day, Italians refer to an espresso as a caffè.)

These elegant establishments reflected the grandeur of the Renaissance. The famous Caffè Florian opened its doors in Venice's Piazza di San Marco in 1720. Started by Floriano Francesconi under the name Venezia Trionfante, the patrons soon began referring to it as Florian's—the same name used today. It was not long before the entire Piazza di San Marco was occupied by a multitude of caffès.

An early attempt was made in the Caffè della Spaderia to use the Italian coffeehouses to spread radical new ideas, but the Catholic church's inquisitors sent a soldier to the Venetian establishment with the message that the first person entering the coffee shop would be hauled off to a tribunal. Thereafter, the focus shifted from politics to pastries—but not for long.

Venetian coffeehouses became so popular that they were frequented by all classes. To be sure, certain caffès became the enclave of individuals with like tastes. They specialized in particular subjects such as law, poetry, medicine, or trade. So fashionable were these coffeehouses that they became the repositories of public postings—personal cards, notes, and itineraries—so that visitors to the city could inquire as to the whereabouts of those they wished to meet.

In his book *The Venetian Republic*, William Carew Hazlitt provides a beautiful description of Venice's caffès and their contribution to the city's life:

> The origin of coffee and coffee-houses elsewhere is traced to the Levant, where an English traveller, Sir Henry Blunt [*sic*], saw them in the earlier part of the reign of Charles I.; and nowhere should such institutions have obtained an earlier footing than here. They have been sufficiently abundant since the middle of the eighteenth century, and no establishment in Europe ever acquired such world-wide celebrity as that kept by Florian, the friend of Canova, and the trusted agent and acquaintance of hundreds of persons in and out of the city, who found him an

unfailing source of information about everything and everybody. Persons leaving the city for a time left their cards and addresses and a clue to their movements with him; others coming to it inquired under his roof for tidings of those whom they desired to see; he long concentrated in himself a knowledge more varied and multifarious than that possessed by any individual before or since. Venetian coffee was said to surpass all other, and the article placed before his visitors by Florian was said to be the best in Venice. So cordial was the esteem of the great sculptor for him, that, when Florian was overtaken by gout, he made a model of his leg, that the poor fellow might be spared the anguish of fitting himself with boots. The friendship had begun when Canova was entering on his career, and he never forgot the substantial services which had been rendered to him in the hour of need.

But previously to the days of this famous and almost historical restauranteur, the Council of Ten had been laying their hand on alleged abuses connected with the coffee-houses of the metropolis, which are charged in decrees of the 18th December 1775, and 28th December 1776, with fostering all kinds of corruption and immorality by harbouring women and youths, and remaining open to outrageous hours. An indirect fruit of this mischief was that the principal thoroughfares were thronged all night with loungers of both sexes and that public morals were jeopardised; and the Inquisitors of State were directed to eradicate this social canker.[5]

Venice's prominence as a city of trade and coffee became the lubricant for many commercial transactions. But coffee also excelled in bringing together those who were dedicated to more-intellectual pursuits. The great university town of Padua witnessed the emergence of many coffeehouses during the latter part of the eighteenth century. They served as the primary venue for literary, social, and scientific meetings—by 1760 there were at least forty coffee establishments listed in Padua. (Lest we forget, it was in this city that William Harvey, the great physician who descibed the circulatory system, first tried coffee more than 150 years earlier.) Antonio Pedrocchi, a local lemonade vendor, thought he could do a bustling business with students and purchased an old house with a number of rooms precisely for that purpose. Unfortunately, it had no proper basement to make ice, so lemonade was out of the question. Undaunted, he decided to dig a basement himself and, lo and behold, he discovered his house to be standing over the vault of an old church that contained a considerable amount of treasure. Keeping the discovery to himself, Pedrocchi decided to invest his newfound fortune in establishing a great European coffeehouse, which he appropriately named the Caffè Pedrocchi.

Designed by the famous architect Giuseppe Jappelli, an Italian neoclassical architect and engineer, the Caffè Pedrocchi was constructed between 1826 and 1831. The first floor hosted and still hosts the coffeehouse itself,

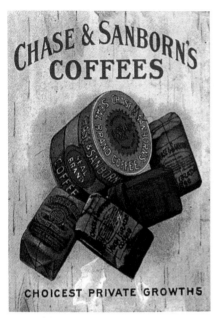

CHASE & SANBORN'S COFFEES

CHOICEST PRIVATE GROWTHS

Chase Sanborn ad.

Gold ram caught in thicket, 2650–2550 BCE. British Museum. *Photograph by Morton Satin, 1992.*

Coffee berries. *Photograph by Morton Satin, 1992.*

Coffee plant. Print from William H. Ukers, *All about Coffee* (New York: Tea and Coffee Trade Journal Company, 1922).

COFFEE ARABICA; LEAVES, FLOWERS AND FRUIT
Painted from nature by M. E. Eaton — Detail sketches show anther, pistil, and section of corolla

Packaged roasted beans. *Photograph by Morton Satin, 2008.*

Early expansion of coffee. From *Theatrum Orbis Terrarum* by Abraham Ortelius (1527–1528).

Expansion of coffee trade to Europe and Asia. From *Theatrum Orbis Terrarum* by Abraham Ortelius (1527–1528).

Ceccanti Espresso poster.

Produits Maxime poster.

Cappiello's Café Martin poster.

Cappiello's classic Arduino poster.

Meunier's Rajah Café poster.

Canned coffee and chicory ad.

Cappiello's Beriot Chicory ad.

Sign of Good Coffee ad.

An espresso being brewed.
Photograph by Morton Satin.

while the upper floor is home to a beautiful room dedicated to the composer Rossini and is currently used for art exhibits. The building is considered to be one of Italy's finest pieces of neoclassical architecture built in the nineteenth century. Among the Caffè Pedrocchi's great historical moments was February 8, 1848, when a university student used the establishment as a base to rouse the student body and local citizenry to march in favor of the Italian Unification (Risorgimento).

Many other Italian cities established famous coffeehouses, particularly Rome, Florence, and Milan.

Coffee's entry into Paris was the result of the diplomatic snub to Ambassador Soliman Aga Mustapha Raca by Louis XIV. Having been dispatched in 1669 to the Parisian court of Louis by Emperor Mehmed IV, the Turkish ambassador had traveled with a considerable entourage and appropriate accoutrements to ensure his comfort during his stay. Among the materials he brought from Constantinople was a sizeable quantity of coffee. In order to establish the correct political pecking order, Louis XIV did not immediately accept the visit from Soliman. To be noticed in the interim, the ambassador, as noted earlier, decided to open his rented home, which he had lavishly decked out in Oriental fashion to show off to the elite of Paris. There he entertained and quietly influenced them while serving them the best of Turkish coffee. It was not long before all things Turkish became the rage in Paris. People dressed up in Turkish costumes topped off with fezzes and openly demanded greater access to the new beverage.

In short order, Pasqua Rosée, who had left London, established Paris's first coffeehouse in 1672. Twenty years earlier he had opened London's first coffeehouse, so he was fully experienced in running such an establishment. Because he was so good at it, he managed to hold a citywide monopoly on coffee until the Sicilian Francesco Procopio dei Coltelli opened Café le Procope in 1686. Here, gentlemen of fashion might gather to drink coffee, that exotic Levantine brew, or eat an elegantly presented sorbet served up by waiters dressed in exotic "Turkish" garb.

In 1689 the Comédie Française settled across the street from the Café le Procope, so dei Coltelli's establishment became known as the quintessential theater café. It attracted a grand mix of notable habitués who delighted visitors. In 1702 Louis, chevalier de Mailly, remarked in *Les Entretiens des Caffés*:

> The cafés are most agreeable places, and ones where one finds all sorts of people of different characters. There one sees fine young gentlemen, agreeably enjoying themselves; there one sees the savants who come to leave aside the laborious spirit of the study; there one sees others whose gravity and plumpness stand in for merit. Those, in a raised voice, often impose silence on the deftest wit, and rouse themselves to praise everything that is to be blamed, and

blame everything that is worthy of praise. How entertaining for those of spirit to see originals setting themselves up as arbiters of good taste and deciding with
an imperious tone what is over their depth![6]

Throughout the eighteenth century, the Procope was the
meeting place of the intelligentsia and many great
writers. Notables such as Voltaire, Rousseau, and
Diderot frequented the Procope, making it arguably the
birthplace of the legendary *Encyclopédie*, the first
modern comprehensive encyclopedia to be published.
Everybody who was anybody made sure they were seen
at the Procope, including the American revolutionaries
Benjamin Franklin, John Paul Jones, and Thomas Jef-
ferson while they were in Paris.

During the French Revolution the conical Phrygian
cap, the symbol of Liberty, was first displayed at the Café
le Procope. Untold numbers of the most prominent in
society were regulars, including Maximilien Robespierre,
Georges Danton, Jean-Paul Marat, Amandine Aurore
Lucile Dupin (better known as George Sand), and Anatole
France. This iconic coffeehouse still stands today and can
be found at 13 rue de l'Ancienne Comédie in Paris.

With the opening of Kolschitzky's Blue Bottle, Viennese coffeehouses began their long journey to world
fame. It was during the eventful year of 1683, with the
Turks at the gates of their beloved city, that Viennese
bakers created crescent-shaped rolls in defiance of their

enemy. Known in Vienna as *kipfel*, these pastries took on greater fame in Italy as the breakfast *cornetto* or in France when re-created as the ubiquitous croissant, available everywhere today in all forms, including the croissant-wich.

Who can visit Vienna without spending an hour in the classic Café Sacher, where waiters will bring you superb coffee accompanied by a perfect slice of the world's most famous chocolate cake, Sacher-Torte?

Thus, coffeehouses soon flourished throughout all the capitals of Europe. They were so successful and became such an integral part of the fabric of European society that even though most of the great coffeehouses were totally destroyed during World War II, a great many of them have been brought back to life to preserve their legend and celebrated atmospheres.

8

Coffee Drives Productivity

I recall one day not very long ago when I attended a technical meeting that was hosted at the impressive facilities of one of our capital's many "Beltway bandits," the private companies located around the asphalt freeway that circumscribes Washington, DC. If you ever take the drive from the Beltway to Dulles International Airport, you will see the lights in their offices burning all night.

The typical employee is young, bright, and brimming with nervous energy. The buildings are as high tech as can be imagined, the meeting rooms equipped with all of the audiovisual and Internet- or satellite-communications facilities befitting such enterprises. During the lunch break, all the meeting participants went down to the cafeteria, which featured a number of cooks preparing scrumptious stir-frys, fresh sushi plates, different pastas, and on and on—an amazing operation for an in-house cafeteria.

Although I was very impressed with the range of freshly cooked foods available to employees, I was not prepared for what awaited me in the refrigerated beverage cabinet. In front of me stood the largest variety of caffeinated energy drinks I had ever seen. Some of the brands on display were All City NRG, Ammo, Amp Overdrive, Arizona Green Tea Energy, Beaver Buzz, Blow, Boo-Koo Energy, Celsius, Daredevil, Fixx, Jolt Cola, Rage, Red Bull, Rockstar Roasted, Spike Shooter, Viso Energy Vigor, Who's Your Daddy, and Xyience Xenergy. There was a greater variety of energy drinks here than I had ever seen in any supermarket. All these drinks were combinations of caffeine and taurine. Surprisingly, Red Bull—the drink that will purportedly give you wings—had one of the lowest caffeine contents of the whole group, approximating the same as that of a regular cup of coffee. Some of the beverages on display had five times the amount of caffeine you would find in a cup of coffee.

It was clear to me why I had seen so many wide-eyed and bushy-tailed young employees. The entire staff was wired on caffeine! No wonder the lights never went out around the Beltway! It was clear proof of the notion that caffeine improves productivity.

Humans have long resorted to various alkaloids as

stimulants such as kola leaves and nuts—they still do in many countries in Africa and the South Pacific. However, very few people today munch on the fruits or nuts of caffeine-based plants. Most of us get our caffeine from drinking coffee or tea, or, to a lesser extent, from the new generation of energy drinks or by taking caffeine tablets. The latest research appears to confirm that caffeine does indeed improve productivity and reduces mental fatigue. It showed that the administration of caffeine improved the performance of tasks by enhancing central nervous activity without increasing the sense of fatigue.[1]

Caffeine has a number of effects on the body, but the one that is relevant to enhancing alertness and reducing fatigue is that it blocks adenosine receptors in the brain. Because of the similarity of the caffeine molecule to adenosine, it works by fooling your brain into thinking it is adenosine—a neuro-modulator and sleep inducer. When the activity of adenosine is reduced, a much greater rate of neuron firing occurs, resulting in increased focus and concentration.

The problem is that caffeine tolerance develops fairly quickly, which means that you start producing more adenosine in response to the amount of caffeine ingested. Therefore, in order to get the same original effect, you have to consume more and more caffeine. This appears not to have deterred most coffee drinkers. Some of the greatest minds of the past four hundred years have sworn by coffee and continued to drink it all their lives.

Caffeine and adenosine. (© Morton Satin, 2008.)

One way to prevent a buildup of coffee tolerance is to take a break now and then from drinking it. Without caffeine to minimize adenosine blockage, the adenosine levels drop back. The weekends are thus a perfect time to cut out or minimize coffee consumption or to drink decaffeinated coffee.

Coffee affects alertness in a number of ways. For those people doing repetitive tasks, coffee can level out the everyday swings from sleepiness to alertness. This is perfect because you lose your drowsiness so that you can continue doing your work. And even if your high level of alertness goes down a wee bit, it's of no great significance if you're doing repetitive tasks. Thus, coffee is perfect for those who work on a production line.

On the other hand, if you are out there to produce conceptual blockbusters, shift paradigms, and demonstrate peak creativity, any loss of alertness is not what you want. You would want to be at your absolute peak of alertness and mental consciousness. Therefore, the best time to drink coffee is when you are already alert so that it can provide an added burst of consciousness. Then again, many other factors contribute to that period of time when your thought processes are at their very peak, such as sound and light.

The high acceptability of coffee for most consumers and its extraordinary ability to improve an individual's alertness inevitably led opportunistic entrepreneurs to come up with improved ways to market it. In the United States a great deal of creative commercial development focused upon coffee. The first prepackaged coffee, sold in stoneware pots and jars, appeared in New York in 1790, along with the first US advertisement for coffee, which appeared appropriately enough in the *New York Daily Advertiser*. Two years later, New York's famous coffeehouse, the Tontine, was opened.

The first cargos of coffee in American ships arrived from Mocha, Yemen, in Salem, Massachusetts, in 1804, followed by shipments directly from Brazil. By 1825 coffee was introduced in Hawaii, and America had its first coffee-related patent—for a coffeepot, issued to Mr. Lewis Martelley. By the middle of the nineteenth century, Americans were each drinking over five pounds of coffee per year, just about the highest per capita consumption in the world. One-third of the world's coffee was being imported to the United States. Coffee had become more available and cheaper because of its production in Haiti (Saint Domingue) and Martinique.

Then the first commercial coffee brands began to appear. The first ground-roasted packaged coffee was Osborn's Celebrated Prepared Java Coffee, which appeared in 1860. This was followed after the Civil War with the first national brand, Arbuckle's Ariosa, introduced in 1873. It was a variant of the coffee John Arbuckle first introduced to the trade in Pittsburgh eight years earlier. Sold in paper bags, this made coffee preparation much more convenient. This brand eventually became Yuban.

During and after the Civil War, coffee technology continued to advance through a series of patents that were issued to inventor Jabez Burns from 1864 to 1872 for coffee roasters, coolers, mixers, and grinders. The Boston-based coffee roasters Chase and Sanborn started to package and sell roasted coffee in sealed containers.

After the Civil War, America began to exploit its wealth of natural resources by putting the mass of its new immigrants to work. At the dawn of the twentieth century, coffee fueled their unparalleled productivity. In the sweatshops of New York City's Lower East Side, under oftentimes unbearable conditions, workers would cut, assemble, and sew more garments if they were charged up

Early Maxwell House ad. (Originally appeared in the *Saturday Evening Post*.)

with coffee. Coffee was often supplied freely or at subsidized rates—all with the goal of keeping employees working at high outputs throughout their long shifts—and on into overtime whenever necessary. How could anybody complain about free or cheap coffee?

It was not long before coffee became the national beverage that accompanied nearly everyone throughout the day. We awoke to the thought of having a good cup of coffee to start things off, we sipped the hot brew throughout the day, and we often finished the evening meal with a good cup of coffee. This was the case whether you were a New York government employee, a West Coast fisherman, a worker in a Chicago packinghouse, or a cowboy driving cattle a thousand miles to the railhead.

Coffee brands such as Maxwell House, Hills Brothers, and Folgers became household names. Advertisements appeared everywhere. There were even advertisements that tried to turn people off coffee, such as the Postum ads condemning coffee. (Postum was a grain-based coffee substitute that gained great popularity in the early part of the twentieth century.) A significant amount of research went into brewing the perfect cup of coffee, but none could compare to the efforts of Samuel Cate Prescott.

Born on a small farm in New Hampshire in 1872, Prescott became interested in science at a very early age and graduated from the Massachusetts Institute of Technology (MIT) at age twenty-two. His scientific interests were eclectic, with his expertise mainly focused on microbiology, food science, and public health issues. During World War I, he served as a major in the US Army Sanitary Corps and was soon promoted to the rank of colonel.

After the war, Prescott joined MIT and became one of the world's outstanding food scientists. His fame at MIT soon brought him to the attention of the National Coffee Roasters Association, an industry trade group that was looking at better ways of making coffee in order to expand their sales. Because they felt that coffee technology was in need of a stronger science base, they approached Prescott and promised him a forty-thousand-dollar grant to establish a full, state-of-art coffee research laboratory complete with staff if he would discover the most scientific method of producing the perfect cup of coffee. It was an offer that Prescott could not refuse.

In 1920 he set about testing every possible way to make coffee. Recruiting young ladies from around the campus, he turned them into an effective "taste panel" and started to ply them with every permutation and combination of coffee he could think of. His research went on for three years before he found what he felt was the perfect method. His results, published in 1923, demonstrated that the drip method works best, preferably with freshly ground coffee in a glass or ceramic pot, with the water held just below boiling—almost the same method developed by German housewife Melitta Bentz more than a decade earlier, but more on Bentz later.

The National Coffee Roasters Association immediately began to publicize Prescott's method, and the taste of the typical "American" cup of coffee was established.

The professor's discovery was very timely. Soon, prohibition would become part of the American fabric and folks would no longer be able to linger over a beer. Since drinking coffee wasn't a crime, friends, business associates, students, and anyone wanting to take a break could sit down over a cup of hot, aromatic, and comforting coffee. Coffee consumption soared. North American per capita consumption almost doubled between 1880 and 1920 to sixteen pounds per capita.

By 1933 coffee became one of the most advertised products. Together, Standard Brands and General Foods spent almost 3 million dollars on radio spots alone. Some of the most famous radio shows owed their start to coffee advertising, including the *Edgar Bergen and Charlie McCarthy Show*. Coffee became an everyday necessity. Some diners used coffee to attract truckers by offering free seconds.

Although many modern coffee elitists decry the typical American coffee taste of the twentieth century, they are really only referring to the coffee of the post-1960s era. Until that time, good American coffee had a great taste wherever it was served. The taste and aroma was so rich that, after the war, the Japanese who successfully copied the best that every other country had to offer were able to perfectly mimic great American coffee. In fact, today some of Japan's better hotels are the only place where you can find great, old-fashioned American coffee.

The decline in the taste of American coffee was due to a number of factors. GIs, returning from service after World War II, had developed a taste for the instant coffee that was part of their regular field rations. It was not so much that they loved instant coffee but that they no longer demanded great-tasting coffee. Having such a large influx of consumers who were tight on cash and not too critical paved the way for coffee's decline in taste.

Perhaps the worst thing that happened to American coffee was the result of our continual desire to get more value for our money. It all began when the waiter or waitress went from table to table offering to top off the cup. It did not take long before every roadside diner and then every restaurant began offering the bottomless cup. That's right, the bottomless cup was the final nail in the coffin of the great American cup of coffee. Since hardly anyone can resist a bargain, nearly everyone went along with the idea.

When you stop to think about it, it makes perfect sense. How can somebody ever make a profit using good-quality coffee while allowing the customer to consume as much as he or she wants without charging extra? How could anyone afford to pour out three cups of the same quality coffee and make the same profit as he previously made serving only one cup? The only way that can be done is if the coffee cost one-third as much.

In short order, Americans dutifully sacrificed quality for quantity until the average cup of coffee was pretty awful.

In concert with the poor quality of coffee that consumers found in diners or restaurants, many of the large coffee manufacturers began to reduce the quality of their coffee, believing that consumers would not notice the difference. The consumption of coffee at restaurants did not drop, so why should it drop for home consumption? Much more robusta coffee replaced arabica in the nationally marketed blends. As soon as the price of coffee began to drop in step with its quality, the supermarkets began demanding ever-cheaper blends. Once such a trend began, it was only the last blend that became the flavor standard, so in small incremental steps, coffee quality steadily spiraled downward as pricing pressures were applied.

The ultimate blow came when supermarket chains decided to use coffee as a loss leader. Loss leaders are products sold at cost or even at a loss for the sole purpose of bringing customers into the store so that they will buy the rest of their weekly orders there. The supermarkets had done this with white bread and repeated it with coffee—two essential food commodities. The pressure to produce these as cheaply as possible radically changed the quality of the products and also dramatically reduced the consumer's perception of their value. After all, could a twenty-four-ounce loaf of bread selling for twenty-five cents have any nutritional value at all?

Another problem with coffee was the extended distribution chain it had to endure and the technology that was used to manage it. Once roasted, coffee oils quickly become rancid due to oxygen in the air. In order to prevent this, coffee was placed in cans strong enough to be placed under a vacuum that removed as much air as possible. Placing coffee under a vacuum sucked a great deal of the volatile flavors out of the product, thereby reducing both the aroma and the taste.

If all that was not enough to destroy the taste of coffee, any vestiges of quality left were removed by the most common method of making coffee at home—percolation. Chrome electric coffee percolators could be found in every home. Massachusetts inventor James Mason received a patent for the coffee percolator on December 26, 1865. This type of appliance made extraction easy, but the repeated refluxing of the beverage through the depleted grounds made for a horrid drink, acceptable only if the initial coffee quality was very high.

Coffee consumption began to take a nosedive. Between 1950 and 1984, the per capita consumption of coffee declined by almost 40 percent, finally stabilizing at approximately ten pounds of green coffee beans per person per year. In order to stay awake, a number of people who had gotten used to the shot of caffeine drank alternative caffeinated beverages instead, more than quadrupling the consumption of these beverages. By the 1980s, carbonated soft drinks had replaced coffee as

America's number one beverage. People were getting their caffeine boost from Coke, Pepsi, or Mountain Dew instead of coffee.

Coffee, that quintessential American brew—the cup that comforted all Americans since the Boston Tea Party was destined to become a footnote in America's beverage history. Things would likely have remained that way were it not for the intervention of one individual who, as we shall soon see, hailed from the tiny country that figured so centrally in the history of coffee—that lowland country that first spread coffee around the world—the Netherlands.

9

Coffee Art and Advertising

Whether as romantic illustrations of the exotic origins of coffee or paintings of café society, alluring images have long been used in depicting the aura that surrounds coffee. Nowhere was this more apparent than in commercial art.

In promoting espresso coffee, the original imagery was a reflection of speed and industry. One of the most famous coffee posters of all time was commissioned by the company Victoria Arduino, a manufacturer of supremely elegant yet functional espresso machines. The company hired a brilliant graphic artist from Tuscany named Leonetto Cappiello (1875–1942), whose work became the basis of their advertising campaign. It was his sensuality and evocative artwork that thrust Victoria Arduino's espresso maker into the art nouveau limelight. (See color insert.)

Everybody knows the 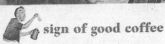 **sign of good coffee**

Perfect timing for a neighborly invitation. The long cold miles ahead will seem shorter after a heart-warming cup of truly good coffee . . . full-bodied, fragrant Maxwell House. The *only* coffee with that famous "Good to the Last Drop" flavor. Behind that finer flavor, there's a secret . . . a closely guarded recipe for certain fine coffees, and how to blend them for *more* richness, *more* mellowness, *more* deeply satisfying goodness. Because it offers the *best* in coffee drinking pleasure, *more* people buy and enjoy Maxwell House than any other brand of coffee—*at any price!*

Now in instant form too!

Products of General Foods

TUNE IN . . . "Father Knows Best" . . . delightful family comedy
starring Robert Young . . . NBC, Thursday nights

Maxwell House . . . the one coffee with that "Good to the Last Drop" flavor!

Rewarding the Mailman ad.

When Christmas brings back familiar faces...

Maxwell House says "Welcome Home!"

● When the Christmas firelight flickers on happy holiday reunions...the friendly aroma of Maxwell House Coffee fills the air with a spirit of welcome. This world-famous coffee, bought and enjoyed by *more* people than any other brand in the world, has been—for many years—a symbol of warm hospitality and gracious living!

No pains are spared, from bean to cup, to give Maxwell House that *extra* flavor richness that means *extra* enjoyment.

A Product of General Foods

GOOD TO THE LAST DROP!

Choice Latin-American coffees are skill-fully selected for flavor . . . mellow-ness . . . vigor . . . then expertly blended for *complete* coffee satisfaction. Radiant Roasting develops the full strength and flavor—*evenly* . . . *thoroughly!* In victory bag or vacuum jar, Maxwell House is now —as always—"Good to the Last Drop!"

★ JOIN THE GIRLS IN NAVY BLUE! WAVES are needed *urgently!* Now's the time to help our Navy do their big job! When our fighting men come home—you can be proud of the help you gave them!

IT'S MAXWELL HOUSE COFFEE TIME ON THE AIR, TOO . . . THE NEW FRANK MORGAN SHOW . . . NBC, THURSDAY NIGHT

Christmas coffee ad. (Originally appeared in the *Saturday Evening Post*.)

It's Maxwell House Coffee Time ad. (Originally appeared in the *Saturday Evening Post* on October 7, 1944.)

The Maxwell House label became an icon of American food culture. These old Maxwell House ads depict the warmth and comfort of coffee.

How many Western movies have we seen with cowboys sitting around a campfire drinking coffee? Aside from instant, cowboy coffee is the easiest type to make. The coffee is brewed in a standard cooking kettle over a fire without anything else—no filters, no tools, nothing. That's why it's a favorite of cowboys and campers. Simply heat the water to boiling, add the ground coffee, and stir. When the grounds settle, drink. For a more authentic blend, add broken egg shells, as they absorb some of the bitter oils.

Cowboy coffee. (© Morton Satin, 2008.)

Finally, here is my favorite image of relaxing with the paper and a good cup of coffee.

A relaxing cup of coffee.
(Used under license from FeaturePics.com.)

10

Coffee Trivia and Coffee Quotes

BACH'S "COFFEE CANTATA"

> Mmm! how sweet the coffee tastes,
> more delicious than a thousand kisses,
> mellower than muscatel wine.
> Coffee, coffee I must have,
> and if someone wishes to give me a treat,
> ah, then pour me out some coffee!

This is a translation of the libretto written by C. F. Henrici for Johann Sebastian Bach's "Coffee Cantata." Bach composed the cantata from 1732 to 1734 for a performance by the famous Leipzig Collegium Musicum, which was started in 1702 by Georg Philipp Telemann and was located at Zimmerman's coffeehouse in the center of the old town. It was literally unthinkable

Bach's "Coffee Cantata." Libretto by Christian Friedrich Henrici, Cantata BMV 211. Composed for performance by Bach's Collegium at Zimmerman's Coffee House, Leipzig, between 1732 and 1734.

for any respectable musician traveling through Leipzig to avoid paying a visit to Bach and enjoying an evening of music with him. The concerts at Zimmerman's were generally put together at the last minute. Thus they were rarely advertised and normally bereft of printed programs. Everyone in town simply knew that on Friday evenings, all one had to do was show up at Zimmerman's and there would be a concert by Bach and his associates of the Collegium Musicum. One such concert was a tongue-in-cheek celebration of coffee, including a farcical proclamation about who should or should not be allowed to drink it. He called it "Kafee-Kantate," or "Coffee Cantata."

In the cantata, a father is highly annoyed that his daughter is crazy about coffee and sets about ridding her of the addictive habit. He threatens her with all sorts of deprivations, but she remains adamant and refuses to give up her favorite beverage. When the father threatens the withdrawal of a marriage offer, she relents and tells him she would rather have a husband than her coffee. But it doesn't end there as Bach adds a trio where the daughter insists that any marriage contract she enter into will include her right to drink as much coffee as she likes.

Generally, little-known, insignificant facts may not appear to be particularly relevant, but it is often the obscure details that add color, interest, and scope to any subject.

KOPI LUWAK

The world's most expensive coffee is made from coffee berries that have been eaten by the Asian Palm Civet (*Paradoxurus hermaphroditus*) and passed through the cat's digestive tract. That's right—pussycat poop! The civet's digestion process breaks down the berries, but the beans inside pass through undigested. This unusual phenomenon takes place on the islands of Sumatra, Java, and Sulawesi in Indonesia as well as in the Philippines and Vietnam with the local varieties of the Palm Civet cat.[1]

Kopi Luwak sells for $150 to $600 per pound, mainly in Japan and the United States. In April 2008 the brasserie of Peter Jones department store in London's Sloane Square started selling a blend of Kopi Luwak and Blue Mountain called Caffè Raro for £50 a cup. A spokesman for the store purportedly said, "These rare coffees have been slowly hand roasted for around twelve minutes to ensure that we maximize the potential of each coffee. More importantly, any residual dung is carefully washed away!"[2]

WORLD COFFEE TRADE

As a commodity traded on world markets, coffee is second only to oil and exceeds, in value, all other commodities such as coal, meat, wheat, and sugar. Over the past ten years, coffee bean prices in the United States have varied between eighteen and thirty cents per ounce.[3] The prices fluctuate with supply, which is driven by factors such as the weather in coffee-producing countries and the impact of new producers into the international market. Wholesale and retail food prices are generally more stable than commodity prices.

COFFEE PRODUCTION

The top five producers of coffee in the world are Brazil (33 percent), Vietnam (11 percent), Colombia (9 percent), Indonesia (8.3 percent), and Mexico (3.7 percent).[4]

COFFEE CONSUMPTION

The per capita consumption (pounds per year) in the fifteen countries that consume the most coffee in the world is:

Norway	24
Finland	22
Denmark	21
Sweden	17
Netherlands	16
Switzerland	15
Germany	13

Austria	12
Belgium	11
France	9
Italy	7
United States	7
Canada	5
Australia	4
Japan	3

As a nation, the United States is the world's largest consumer of coffee, importing more than 20 percent of all coffee exported. On an individual basis, however, Americans drink only a third of what the Nordics do.[5]

COFFEE YIELD

An acre of coffee trees can produce up to ten thousand pounds of coffee cherries or approximately two thousand pounds of beans after hulling or milling.[6]

COFFEE DISTRIBUTION

The world's busiest transfer point for coffee is the port of Hamburg, Germany.[7]

COFFEE DAY

October 1 is the official Coffee Day in Japan. (There is no truth to the rumor that for three months prior to this day, Asian Palm Civic cats go into hiding for fear of being force-fed coffee berries.)

MELITTA BENTZ

Melitta Bentz was a German housewife from Dresden who invented the first coffee filter. She wanted to brew a better cup of coffee without the bitterness caused by conventional brewing. She took a conical cup and lined it with a filter paper. She added the ground coffee and poured boiling water through it. The resulting brew was just what she wanted. On July 8, 1908, the conical coffee filter and filter paper were patented, and six months later Melitta and her husband, Hugo, started the Melitta Bentz Company.

INSTANT COFFEE

Japanese American chemist Satori Kato invented the first instant coffee in 1901; the process was commercialized within five years. Instant coffee enjoyed the height of its popularity in the 1970s, when more than 200 million pounds of product were sold annually in the United States. Today, about 15 percent of the coffee consumed in the United States is instant, prepared either at home, in offices, or in public vending machines.[8]

BOSTON TEA PARTY

A prelude to the American Revolution, the Boston Tea Party in December 1773 was the pivotal event that began the shift in America to become a coffee-drinking nation. Up until then tea was a more popular beverage, but the heavy tax on it imposed by the British brought about the adoption and popularity of coffee as the number one consumed beverage in America. Appropriately, the Boston Tea Party was planned in the Green Dragon coffeehouse.

PRUSSIAN COFFEE REVOLT

In the 1780s, Frederick the Great issued a coffee manifesto, asserting that all citizens must drink beer instead of coffee. A heavy tax was imposed on coffee. Coffee drinking continued but as a luxury afforded only by the wealthy. In 1781 Frederick tried to create a monopoly by prohibiting coffee roasting except in royal establishments. Some tried using coffee substitutes, such as chicory, but they could not take the place of real coffee. In 1785 a coffee revolt broke out in Prussia and two years later, Frederick's successor decided to lower the tax, thus ending all restrictions.

MILITARY RATIONS

In 1832 President Andrew Jackson introduced sugar and coffee into the US Army diet, replacing the customary allotments of rum, whiskey, or brandy.

During the American Civil War, Union soldiers who were expected to prepare their own food were issued four pounds of ground roasted coffee per one hundred rations—enough coffee to brew themselves four to five strong cups a day. And they were given another choice— they could take ten pounds of green coffee beans in case they wanted to roast their own.

During World War I troops were allotted 1.12 ounces of roasted and ground coffee per day—enough for two to three cups per day. For troops in the trenches, instant coffee was provided for the first time.

The K-rations of World War II were broken up into breakfast, dinner, and supper units, with only the breakfast ration providing coffee in the form of instant coffee—five grams, enough for two cups.

MACCHIATO

The term *macchiato* stems from the Italian word *macchia*, which means stain. Espresso macchiato is a cup of espresso that is "stained" with a dollop of steamed milk, whereas latte macchiato is a cup of steamed milk "stained" with a shot of espresso.

COFFEE CRÈMA

Crèma is the gold-colored foam of coffee oils that covers a shot of espresso. Crèma is a weak emulsion that forms a layer that helps retain the aroma and flavor of the espresso. Good crèma lasts a few minutes before breaking up and settling.

CAPPUCCINO OFFICIAL STANDARD

According to Italy's National Institute for Italian Espresso, cappuccino is made up as follows:

The ingredients are 125 ml (4 ¼ oz.) milk, no warmer than 3–5°C (37–41°F), containing a minimum of 3.2% protein and 3.5% fat (whole milk) and a 25 ml (0.85 oz.) shot of hot espresso coffee, made using 7 g (¼ oz.) ground coffee.

Add coffee to a 150–160ml (6 oz.) capacity

ceramic cup. Froth milk with steam to a temperature of 55°C (131°F), and add to cup. Add sugar if needed and stir gently.

CAFFEINE

Most of the world's purified caffeine—used to fortify soft drinks and used in over-the-counter medicines—is a by-product of the coffee decaffeination process or is extracted from poor-quality coffee beans and tea leaves.

DARK ROAST

Dark-roasted coffees actually have less caffeine than medium roasts. The longer a coffee is roasted, the more caffeine is destroyed during the process.

CAFFEINE CONTENT OF BEVERAGES (APPROXIMATE AVERAGES)

Espresso (1 oz.)	60 mg
Drip coffee (8 oz.)	145 mg
Brewed coffee (8 oz.)	105 mg
Instant coffee (8 oz.)	85 mg
Decaf brewed (8 oz.)	3 mg
Decaf instant (8 oz.)	2 mg

CAFFEINE INFUSIONS

Even though tea contains twice as much caffeine as coffee, you produce between five to ten times the amount of brewed tea than brewed coffee per pound. The end result is that a cup of tea contains only about 25 percent the amount of caffeine as a cup of coffee.

WAKE UP AND SMELL THE BEANS

Recently, researcher Han-Seok Seo and his colleagues at the Department of Food and Nutrition at Seoul National University looked at the effects of sniffing the aroma of freshly roasted coffee beans.[9] Using rats that were stressed out through sleep deprivation, the researchers evaluated the effects of the aroma by performing genetic and protein analyses on brain tissue. They compared the results with other rats that were sleep deprived but not exposed to the roasted coffee bean aroma and determined that the aroma influenced responses in rat brains stressed by sleep deprivation at the chromosomal level— that is, thirteen genes were found to be different between the stressed-with-coffee aroma and the stressed-only rats. They also found one antioxidant protein that was produced at a higher level among the stressed-with-coffee aroma group.

BEETHOVEN'S COFFEE

Beethoven was meticulous in preparing his coffee, using precisely sixty beans per cup, although there is no truth to the story that as the last four beans were counted, he exclaimed "Ta, ta, ta, taaaaa!"

COFFEE QUOTES FROM FAMOUS PEOPLE

Abraham Lincoln (1809–1865, sixteenth president of the United States)

"If this is coffee, please bring me some tea; but if this is tea, please bring me some coffee."

Oliver Wendell Holmes Sr. (1809–1894, physician and writer)

"The morning cup of coffee has an exhilaration about it which the cheering influence of the afternoon or evening cup of tea cannot be expected to reproduce."

Honoré de Balzac (1799–1850, French novelist and playwright)

"Coffee falls into your stomach, and straightway there is a general commotion. Ideas begin to move like the battalions of the Grand Army of the battlefield, and the battle takes place. Things remembered arrive at full gallop, ensuing to the wind. The light cavalry of comparisons deliver a magnificent deploying charge, the artillery of logic hurry up with their train and ammunition, the shafts of which start up like sharpshooters. Similes arise, the paper is covered with ink; for the struggle commences and is concluded with torrents of black water, just as a battle with powder."

Alexander Pope (1688–1744, eighteenth-century English poet)

"Coffee, which makes the politicians wise,
And see through all things with his half-shut eyes."

T. S. Eliot (1888–1965, poet, dramatist, and literary critic)
From "The Love Song of J. Alfred Prufrock"

"I have measured out my life with coffee spoons."

Jonathan Swift (1667–1745, satirist, essayist, political pamphleteer)

"Coffee makes us severe, and grave, and philosophical."

Ronald Reagan (1911–2004, fortieth president of United States)

"Actually, this seems to be the basic need of the human heart in nearly every great crisis—a good hot cup of coffee."

Lord Byron (1788–1824, English Romantic poet and satirist)

"'Tis pity wine should be so deleterious, for tea and coffee leave us much more serious."

Dave Barry (b. 1947, American writer and humorist)

"Eating rice cakes is like chewing on a foam coffee cup, only less filling."

Bill Gates (b. 1955, founder of Microsoft)

"Television is not real life. In real life people actually have to leave the coffee shop and go to jobs."

Lady Nancy Astor (1879–1964, first woman to serve as a British member of Parliament) to Sir Winston Churchill (1874–1965, prime minister)

Astor: "If I were your wife, I would put poison in your coffee."

Churchill: "And if I were your husband, I would drink it."

Jean-Anthelme Brillat-Savarin (1755–1826, French gourmand)

"It is the duty of all papas and mammas to forbid their children to drink coffee, unless they wish to have little dried-up machines, stunted and old at the age of twenty. . . . I once saw a man in London, in Leicester Square, who had been crippled by immoderate indulgence in coffee; he was no longer in any pain, having grown accustomed to his condition, and had cut himself down to five or six cups a day."

Prince Talleyrand (1754–1838, French diplomat)

"Suave molecules of Mocha stir up your blood, without causing excess heat; the organ of thought receives from it a feeling of sympathy; work becomes easier and you will sit down without distress to your principal repast which will restore your body and afford you a calm, delicious night."

Sir James Mackintosh (1765–1832, Scottish jurist, politician, and historian)

"The powers of a man's mind are directly proportioned to the quantity of coffee he drinks."

PART 3

Coffee's Renaissance in a New World

11

The Americanization of European Cafés

In the midst of the downward trend in coffee quality, a thirty-five-year-old Dutchman emigrated to San Francisco in 1955 and took a job with coffee importers E. A. Johnson & Co. The man's name was Alfred Peet and he hailed from Alkmaar, a small city in northern Holland that was renowned for its traditional cheese markets. His father had a small coffee-roasting business where Alfred worked until soldiers of the Third Reich swept into Holland in May 1940. In short order, twenty-year-old Alfred was sent to Frankfurt, where he was forced into labor for the Third Reich as a lathe operator.

When the war was over, Peet emigrated to London where he joined the Lipton Tea Company. In the fashion of many of his countrymen, he soon set out for the Dutch colony of Indonesia, continuing his work in the tea business. Apparently fond of the Pacific and looking for an interesting place to put down his roots, Alfred Peet moved to San Francisco and brought his experience with coffee and tea to E. A. Johnson.

He was dismayed with both the quality of coffee he could purchase in the restaurants as well as the poor quality of the beans being imported by his employer. Occasionally there are times when taking a stand against what is considered to be standard marketing wisdom pays off. Peet felt that the time was right to introduce a higher-quality coffee to the Bay Area. This not only meant that the taste, aroma, and body of the coffee would change, but also the way in which it was consumed. As in Europe, there would no longer be a bottomless cup. Quality coffee is not cheap and the consumers would have to pay for it. In 1966 Alfred Peet took a risk by leaving his job and opening his first shop.

On April Fools' Day, Peet's Coffee and Tea Inc. threw open its doors on the corner of Walnut and Vine streets in Berkeley, a venue perfectly suited for young agitators who wanted nothing more than to be different. The town had so many nonconformists, it was impossible to tell one from another. And here was Peet's Coffee and Tea Inc. producing wonderful aromas from his freshly roasted beans and strong, tasty coffee. His coffee would give drinkers a buzz and allow them to stay up all night basking in the aroma of patchouli oil and listening to the chanting of anti-war folksingers and anti-establishment poets.

Peet's was an immediate success, which, in retrospect, should not appear odd. In countries like Italy, the adherence to traditional quality is sacrosanct. They almost never change anything because they do not want to be the ones held responsible for reducing quality. I recall visiting a Parmesan cheese production establishment near Parma and speaking to the owner. He told me that the only change they had introduced in the last three hundred years was to change their source of sea salt used in the brining baths because the new source had fewer impurities. They even used the same unit of temperature (degrees Réaumur—a temperature unit developed in 1730) in the production process. Reducing the quality of the cheese is the last thing on their minds. That is why Italian products are admired the world over. That is also why they are expensive.

When Alfred Peet decided to bring back higher-quality coffee, there was a large market simply waiting just for that. It was not long before great lines of people were waiting outside his shop, anxious to try his gourmet coffee. While in the coffee shop, Alfred would not hesitate to scold those customers who did not know how to make coffee properly. He was a fastidious Dutchman singularly dedicated to renewing coffee's reputation and status.

Aside from buying higher-quality coffee beans, Peet roasted them darker than mass-produced brands. This was not unusual because the better varieties of coffee are generally mild in flavor and some or all of the beans have to be heavily roasted in order to give it a bit of a bite. This bite is not comparable to the harshness experienced with lower-quality coffee but is the result of careful roasting to bring out peak flavors and acidity.

The success of Peet's Coffee and Tea, Inc. encouraged a great many other small entrepreneurs to open up coffee establishments featuring freshly roasted, high-quality beans from all over the world. Alfred Peet delivered the rebirth of good coffee in America. Gourmet stores started carrying coffee from exotic locations that had been roasted in small establishments all around America. Many of these were run by amateurs wanting to get in on the beginning of a trend. There is simply no replacement for dedication to an ideal, so quality coffee soon became much more widely available.

In order to provide small-scale coffee roasters with some critical mass, a small group met and created a specialty coffee trade association in 1982. Since then, the Specialty Coffee Association of America has become the largest coffee association in the world, with more than two thousand individual members from every aspect of the coffee business. The association is international and includes members from most of the coffee-producing countries as well as from many consuming countries.

In the Pacific Northwest—notably Vancouver, British Columbia—good-quality coffee was always available. From humble beginnings in 1894, a small company called Murchie's opened its doors in order to import quality teas and the very best arabica coffee beans from some of the world's most exotic places. From the very beginning, it always had a reputation for quality, and people traveled hundreds of miles to get their supplies there. This was the case with Seattle writer Gordon Bowker. So, once a month, he would drive the 140 miles north to get the coffee he wanted—that's devotion.

But traveling 140 miles every month and being forced to go through a vigilant border crossing every time became a bit tiring. Bowker came up with the idea of opening a shop and roasting his own coffee—an idea which he shared with his two friends—Jerry Baldwin and Zev Siegl. In search of a model upon which to base a shop, Siegl decided to travel down to San Francisco to reconnoiter the scene. It did not take long before he came across Peet's establishment. He checked it out and immediately saw the possibilities.

Siegl returned home to Seattle and reported what he saw to his friends. The three of them decided to visit Alfred Peet and ask his assistance in setting up their dream operation. Peet eventually agreed to give them the direction and technical help they needed and also to supply them with his coffee for their retail needs.

In 1971 each invested $1,350 and borrowed another $5,000 from the bank to open their Seattle store in Pike Place Market. In picking a name, they thought that a nautical moniker would be suitable and after a few

cracks at it chose the name Starbucks in honor of Starbuck, the first mate on the whaling ship *Pequod* under
the command of Captain Ahab in Herman Melville's
Moby Dick. It was an excellent choice because the name
evoked the romance of the high seas and the exotic
nature of a commodity that hailed from far-off lands. It
was also an easy name to remember. The new company's
logo, designed by a friend, was a twin-tailed mermaid
encircled by the store's name.

The first store had no seats but featured fixtures that
were hand built in Siegl's parent's basement. The first
shop sold the whole-bean coffees shipped up from Peet's
in Berkeley. There was no fresh-brewed coffee available
by the cup, but samples were sometimes prepared for
tasting. The goal was to sell coffee by the pound. Siegl,
the store's only paid employee, wore an old-fashioned
grocer's apron while using a great scoop to dole out the
dark-roasted beans for the customers. In the meantime,
the other two partners took no chances and kept their
regular day jobs, dropping by during lunch times or after
work in order to give Siegl a hand with all the tasks.

Fortunately, the operation was successful from the
start, with sales exceeding all expectations. The three
partners continued to travel to Berkeley to get as much
information as possible on coffee roasting from Alfred
Peet. They soon made enough money and felt confident
enough to buy a used coffee roaster from Holland and
began roasting their own products. It did not take long

before the partners came up with their own blends and flavors and had enough confidence to open a second Starbucks store in 1972. Within a decade, the company added two more stores. Siegl decided to leave the company, and Bowker, although still involved in the ownership, devoted most of his time to other interests. Jerry Baldwin took over the management of the company and functioned as its chief executive.

Around the same time, Howard Schultz, an executive at Hammarplast—a Swedish manufacturer of plastic kitchen housewares—did not understand why a small coffee operation in Seattle was selling more of its drip coffeemakers than the department store giant Macy's. Born in Brooklyn's subsidized Bayview Projects in 1952, Schultz was ambitious and always on the lookout for new opportunities. Starbucks's Seattle operation piqued his curiosity and he decided to pay the company a visit. After one whiff of the roasting beans and one sip of coffee made with freshly ground beans in a Hammarplast coffeemaker, Schultz was taken in. In fact, not only was Schultz taken in, he wanted in.

Schultz was fascinated by the Starbucks commitment to quality and consumer satisfaction. All he could think about was joining Starbucks and expanding the enterprise. As soon as he got back to New York, he contacted Baldwin to discuss the possibilities. Baldwin, Bowker, and Peet were not confident of Schultz's ideas for expansion nor his ability to carry on the Starbucks tradition.

Schultz persisted and eventually overcame their resistance. In September 1982, Howard Schultz took on the responsibility of marketing for Starbucks.

Schultz took on his job with incredible vigor and soon fitted in comfortably with the rest of the staff. His epiphany came during the following year when he visited Milan, Italy, to attend a trade show. While there, he dropped into an espresso bar and witnessed the barista carrying out his trade, serving all types of coffee to the customers. An *espresso* for one, a *lungo macchiato* for another, and a *cappuccino ben caldo* for the third. He was struck by the comfort and ambience of the coffee bar. He dropped by several other bars and saw the same thing. Regardless of whether they were tiny holes in the wall or elegant establishments complete with chandeliers and fine furniture, everyone seemed comfortable and friendly, and each establishment did brisk business. Schultz developed a whole new vision for Starbucks. He was going to bring the coffee bar experience of Italy to the United States. He forgot about the trade show and concentrated instead on the coffee bars. He tried all sorts of Italian coffees and was particularly taken with the *caffè latte*, a glass of steamed milk topped off by a shot of espresso. He now knew his goal in life—nothing less than starting a revolution. Schultz was going to bring a coffee renaissance to America.

Unfortunately, his partners back home did not share that vision. They wanted to buy out Peet's Coffee and

Tea and would have precious little money left over for anything else, especially a whole new business model. After a year of trying to get his idea across, they finally agreed to a test case. In April 1984 Starbucks' sixth store, one in downtown Seattle, became the first to sell beverages. It was a smash hit.

Still, his partners were reluctant to go into the coffee bar business. These differences prompted Schultz to leave Starbucks at the close of 1985 in order to pursue his vision.

With capital raised from investors (including the owners of Starbucks), Schultz opened up his first bar in April 1986 under the name of Il Giornale—the Daily, a typical Italian newspaper name. Some of the Italian affectations were a bit over the top, but it did well, nevertheless. They got rid of some of the excesses, such as the background opera, and in less than half a year Il Giornale was serving more than a thousand customers a day. In short order, Il Giornale opened a second store in downtown Seattle, followed by a third in Vancouver, British Columbia, in April 1987. Schultz was on his way to realizing his dream.

As Schultz was opening his Vancouver shop, the owners of Starbucks decided to sell all of Starbucks except the Peet's operation. Schultz and his board of directors agreed to buy it and completed the deal in August 1987. At the age of thirty-four, Howard Schultz became the president and CEO of Starbucks Corporation.

The next day Schultz set about implementing his vision for Starbucks to go national with the most respected brand name in coffee and for the organization to be recognized for its sense of corporate responsibility. Unfortunately, during the months he had been away running the Il Giornale operation, employee morale had deteriorated. The fact that the previous owners had sold out left the employees wary of their future. Schultz immediately met with them. He knew that building up a relationship of confidence with the employees would have to be a top priority.

Shultz had developed an ambitious plan to open more than a hundred stores within the coming five years and he immediately set about implementing it. All the new Starbucks facilities were to be both a comforting blend of a retail coffee store and an Italian-type espresso bar. Starbucks became a unique profile for beverage retailing.

Starbucks's initial entry into the Chicago market was slow but eventually picked up and by 1990, it became profitable. Bouncing back to the comfort of the West Coast, Oregon became their next market and the coffee drinkers of Portland didn't disappoint. California was a natural market for the type of operation Starbucks had, but the strong presence of Peet's in the San Francisco area drew Starbucks first to Los Angeles. Store openings proceeded at a dizzying pace, but Schultz kept the pressure on, so that within five years they had opened 150 rather than the 125 he had originally envisioned.

Despite initial hiccups in profitability, Starbucks continued to expand. Schultz maintained a close relationship with the employees and was responsible for the implementation of a unique company health program, as well as a plan to provide all employees—not just executives—with stock options. Schultz wanted all the employees to share in the growth and success of Starbucks. While some people thought he was mad, the method to that madness resulted in one of the lowest employee turnover rates in the service industry. The young man, brought up in the poorest of neighborhoods, knew what motivated people and how to gain their loyalty.

When it was decided that Starbucks should go public, their initial IPO in June 1992 was enormously successful. The injection of capital greatly accelerated the expansion of its store operations. Everyone was taking notice, including others who wanted to be in the specialty coffee business. It wasn't long before Starbucks wannabes started to spring up across America.

Starbucks management experimented with different store layouts and different products to attract consumers. Eventually they settled on a consistent layout that provided a comfortable environment where consumers could relax and enjoy their coffee. The beverage menu continued to expand and the number of permutations and combinations of drinks a customer could ask for shot up dramatically. The dedication to coffee went as far as insisting that no employee wear perfume since that might distract from the fresh coffee aroma. Starbucks was also one of the first restaurants to ban smoking for the same reason.

Of particular importance, Starbucks invested heavily in employee training. It was a rarity in the US restaurant or beverage trade, where elsewhere most employees are paid minimum wage and companies have almost nothing invested in their training. At Starbucks, not only was every employee trained how to make coffee properly, but each was taught how to respond to customer needs.

The rest, as they say, is history. Starbucks excelled at purchasing high-quality coffee and having it available to their customers throughout the day. Although a few people criticized the heaviness of their characteristic roast, most savored it, and it maintained their product's identity. They opened up large roasting facilities to keep pace with the growth. Inevitably, Starbucks went international through the licensing of their product bar model to experienced entrepreneurs. In some cases, Starbucks took an active share in the international ventures.

There is absolutely no doubt that Starbucks brought the whole notion of good coffee back to America—no doubt whatsoever. It was more than a matter of coffee, because there were other operations that sold good coffee. In fact, if anyone took the time to go to any Italian neighborhood in any big city, he or she would likely have been able to find an excellent espresso or variations of it. But it was really the vision of one man that reignited America's love for coffee. Today, those big white Starbucks cups with the black and green logo are seen everywhere. Maybe even Howard Schultz couldn't foresee how completely his vision would be realized. There are some entrepreneurs who are driven more by vision and growth than short-term profit, and he appears to be one of them. It is such individuals who are responsible for the great business empires.

As expected, all the latecomers wanted in on the business. The largest conventional coffee processors such as Maxwell House, Folgers, and Nestlé scrambled to get in with their versions of specialty coffees that they sold as whole-bean varieties in national supermarkets. But even in that market, the Starbucks brand started to pay off when it began selling its coffees in supermarkets.

After Schultz stepped down as the CEO of Starbucks in 2000, the number of stores, joint ventures, and licensed operations ballooned from 3,500 to more than 15,000 around the world. Starbucks was no longer a distinctly American phenomenon, but was a world wonder. However, many investors blamed this rapid growth for Starbucks' poor financial performance. On top of that, new competition threatened to cut into Starbucks' future profitability.

Schultz was brought back as chief executive in 2008. It was probably the worst time for someone to retake the helm of a company because the economic downturn placed a real damper on personal indulgences such as high-end coffee. Profits plunged by 69 percent in the last quarter of 2008 and the company had to announce the closure of 900 stores.

Despite those setbacks, it is Schultz's goal to revive Starbucks' innovation and get still closer to its customers. His unparalleled confidence was demonstrated when, in 2009, he unveiled a product that seemed to contravene all our ideas about upscale coffee—an instant coffee called Via Ready Brew. In case any aficionados out there express too much cynicism, let's not forget that it was Howard Schultz who was the architect of coffee's modern renaissance. And no one can diminish the uniqueness of Starbucks' success story.

12

Making Home Brew

The exploding popularity of coffee has generated a new generation of home brewers. Here we will describe the old and new technologies and techniques to make the perfect home brew complete with creamy, rich *schiuma* (foam).

COFFEE GRINDERS

As you'll find when preparing your home coffee brew, the particle size of the grounds is critical. Therefore, it is essential to have your coffee ground in a proper grinder. You can do this in the supermarket as long, as you are confident that the grinder has not been contaminated by somebody who has previously used flavored coffees and

A high-quality grinder. (© Morton Satin, 2008.)

also that the grinder is in good condition and working properly. Don't be afraid to catch a few of the grounds coming out to make sure they're the right size. You should also make certain that not too much coffee dust is being generated in the grinding process.

There are a great many good grinders out on the market. My own personal preference is the burr-type grinder over the blade grinder. Burr grinders are always more expensive than blade-type grinders, but the result is a more uniform grind with far less dust. I specifically use the KitchenAid Pro Line grinder because it has a screw feed mechanism that constantly delivers the beans to the grinder head. Even with that, you have to keep your eye on the grinder to make sure that there are no dead spots that will block the process, so I generally stir the beans with the included brush to make sure that they all get down to the screw feeder. Adjusting the size of grind is a simple turn of the dial.

Approximate grind sizes for various types of coffee:

Grind Size	Brewing Method	Particle Size (microns)	Number of Particles per Coffee Bean
Coarse	French press		
	Percolator		
	Vacuum coffeemaker	600	100–300
Medium	Flat-bottom drip filter maker	480	500–800
Fine	Conical drip filter		
	Moka Expresso maker	350	1,000–3,000
Very fine	Espresso machines	280	3,500
Super fine	Turkish ibrik	751	5,000–30,000

French press grind. (© Morton Satin, 2008.)

TURKISH COFFEE

The great Turkish twentieth-century poet Yahya Kemal said that "coffee has created its own culture in Turkey." For anyone who has spent some time visiting that country, these words ring true. In Turkey, there's no need to specify "Turkish coffee," since all coffee is Turkish coffee.

One style of Turkish ibrik. (© Morton Satin, 2008.)

In Turkey, coffee is not just a casual drink but a national treasure complete with its own history, institutions, rituals, and rules of how and when to drink it. The institutions are, of course, Turkey's innumerable coffeehouses where, if you wish, you might even have your fortune told by a gypsy reading the heavy deposit of coffee grinds sitting at the bottom of your cup.

Turkey was one of the first countries to adopt the

coffee-drinking habit—picked up directly from Yemen, the first country where coffee was grown commercially. Coffeehouses were heavily dispersed throughout the ancient capital of Constantinople. In those days patrons would come in to read public manuscripts while others would engage in games of backgammon. Still others would discuss art and culture while the braver, more outspoken ones would delve into politics as long as no informants were around. Whenever it came time for prayers, the imams and muezzins would scout out the coffeehouses and haul the lazy and irreverent in to the Mosque to ensure their devotion to the Prophet. So pervasive was the habit of drinking coffee that, when the beverage was first introduced in Venice, and then in London and Paris, it was known as the Turkish beverage and eventually as Turkish coffee.

The modern day city of Istanbul is likewise filled with coffeehouses, but instead of patrons engaged in lively conversation and playing backgammon, you will more likely find them watching CNN on wall-mounted TV sets. In a country where the preponderance of coffee drinking has been replaced by tea, the coffeehouses continue as centers of social interaction for students and adults. Whenever in the mood, they drop by their favorite coffee shop confident in the knowledge that they will inevitably find friends or colleagues with whom to chat.

Drinking coffee in Turkey continues to be a richly complex experience involving ritual, tradition, and taste.

Another style of Turkish ibrik. (© Morton Satin, 2008.)

While it may not be practical for readers to drop everything and take a trip to Istanbul, preparing Turkish
coffee is something anyone can learn to do.

The first thing you must have is a Turkish coffeepot,
or an ibrik, but that's not really 100 percent true. If you

wish to make Turkish coffee in the traditional way, you should use an ibrik, but if you just want to make Turkish coffee and are not overly concerned with style or tradition, you can make it in any small saucepan. Just make certain there is enough headspace so the coffee can boil up and settle back down a few times. Turkish coffeepots were originally designed specifically to make Turkish coffee over a bed of coals. The long handle is there to avoid burning hands, and the lip on the rim is designed to pour the coffee. If you're going to buy an ibrik, make certain that you choose the correct size. You might even have to purchase a second one, depending on whether or not you plan to serve company.

An important characteristic of Turkish coffee is that an extremely fine grind is used. Turkish coffee mills closely resemble the same mills that are used for grinding pepper, except that they produce a much finer grain. Of course you can grind the particles down to "Turkish size" using any good coffee mill, including the one at your supermarket (unless it has been contaminated by flavored coffee).

In keeping with tradition, you should also serve your Turkish coffee in the proper cups. Fortunately, Turkish coffee cups have evolved somewhat and now have handles and are available without the expensive filigree and inlaid jewels. In fact, modern Turkish coffee cups closely resemble espresso cups and can easily be replaced by them.

One final note before we get into the preparation of

Turkish coffee. A spice that is often added to Turkish coffee is cardamom. It really does infuse the coffee with a totally different aroma and taste, but adding the spice has to be done very subtly; if not, the cardamom flavor completely takes over the taste of the coffee and you no longer have that alluring fusion of flavors. I would therefore suggest that a cardamom pod be cracked open and a single seed be used per cup to start. Make sure you crush it before adding it to the pot with the coffee. That generally ensures that the cardamom will not overpower the taste and, if the spice is lacking, more can always be added.

The best Turkish coffee is made from freshly roasted beans that are very finely ground just before brewing. A dark roast is always preferable, but if you find it too harsh, a medium roast coffee will also yield a pleasing aroma and flavor. The Turkish grind is considerably finer than espresso—more of a flourlike powder.

To brew Turkish coffee, start by pouring water into the ibrik or coffeepot. You should use one cup of cold water for each cup you are making. Also, use between one and two heaping teaspoons of coffee for each cup. The amount of coffee may be varied to taste, but do not forget there will be a thick layer of coffee grounds left at the bottom of your cup when properly brewing Turkish coffee. Don't overly fill the pot with water. Now add cardamom and sugar to the pot. You are best to start with one level teaspoon of sugar. You can always add more later if need be. (You can omit the sugar if you are concerned with carbohydrates. If you want to add artificial sweetener, do so after the coffee has brewed.) Stir until all the coffee is wetted and sinks to the bottom. Do not stir again as it will dissolve the foam.

Heat the pot on the burner as slowly as you can. The slower the heat, the better it is for the coffee. Make sure you watch it to prevent overflowing when the coffee boils. As soon as the mixture starts to boil, it will froth up quickly. Before the froth boils over, remove the ibrik from the heat and let everything settle down.

Pour some (not all) of the coffee equally between the cups, filling each cup about a quarter to a third of the way. (This ensures that everybody gets a fair share of the foam from the top of the pot. Place the pot back on the burner and continue heating until the coffee boils again (which will be very soon now that it has already boiled). Then distribute the rest of the coffee between the cups.

Since there is no filtering of coffee at any time during this process, you should wait for a minute or so before drinking the coffee. This way, the grounds settle to the bottom of the cup.

FRENCH PRESS METHOD

Many consider the French press method of making coffee the most classic. It is simple and results in a gentle extraction of all the coffee oils. Still others find the taste

A French press. (© Morton Satin, 2008.)

somewhat harsh. As the French say, "Chacun à son goût!"—*To each his own!*

The French coffee press, more simply the coffee press or *cafetiere*, was originally invented in France during the 1850s. James Grierson describes a lovely anecdote of its origin in his article "History of the Cafetiere."[1] An old man from Provence was in the habit of taking a daily stroll up a hill in order to take a break from his nagging wife. He did this come rain or shine and made the experience last longer by carrying his lunch, his coffeepot, and some wood to build a fire upon which to heat the pot. Every day he would reach the hilltop, take a nice rest, build a small fire, eat his lunch, then brew some coffee.

In those days, all coffee was made in the same way— what we know of as cowboy coffee. Coffee grounds would be placed in a pot, water was added, then everything would be placed on an open fire to boil. Inevitably, this resulted in a strong, bitter brew. An old man, he had a tendency of being forgetful, and one day he forgot to add the coffee grounds to his coffeepot before he started boiling it. He realized his mistake, but as he had no wood left to reboil his coffee, he simply added the coffee grounds to the pot without realizing that they would end up floating to the top. He was not sure how to resolve this dilemma.

Luckily, a traveling merchant happened to pass by. Among his wares, the merchant had a small metal screen. When the old man glanced at the screen, he immediately got an idea. He bought the screen from the merchant and carefully fitted it over his open coffeepot. With the help of a little stick, he plunged the metal screen down to the bottom of the pot, pushing the coffee grounds down with it. He then tasted the coffee and was very pleased with it. The merchant asked to try some and pronounced it the best coffee he had ever tasted! Both men decided to open a small shop to produce their new invention and made a small fortune.

The familiar French coffee press we find in stores today was patented in 1929 by the Italian Attilio Calimani. He advanced the design by using a glass jar with a spout, much like a standard glass beaker used in every laboratory, and he constructed a tight-fitting plunger with a filter on the end to press the ground coffee to the bottom of the pot.

In 1958, another Italian, Faliero Bondanini, was granted a patent for an improved version of the cafetiere. This became enormously popular in France and ended up being the standard we see today. Since older versions of the French press lost heat quickly, the designer coffeemaker brand Bodum developed an insulated coffee press. Even more convenient is the integrated electric water heater French press available from Chef's Choice. This type of press is ideal for those who want to simplify the brewing process without sacrificing quality.

In order to make coffee in a French press, start by buying or making coarsely ground coffee beans. Any finely ground particles will go through the screen and end up as sediment in your cup. The finer the grounds, the more difficult it will be to depress the plunger. (If you feel that you may have too many fine grounds in your coarse grind, take your ground coffee and put it through a kitchen sieve, which is about the same porosity as a French press sieve. It may take a bit of time to track one down, but it will be worthwhile.) Remove the top and the filter from the coffeemaker.

Place your coarse coffee grounds in the bottom of the coffeemaker. If you're using a large coffeemaker, start with about 35 g or 5 slightly rounded tbsp of coffee to five 8 oz. cups of water. You can adjust to your preference later. (If using a smaller pot, downsize accordingly, but figure on just slightly more than an 8 oz. cup per rounded tbsp to start.)

Boil your premeasured water, let it cool for half a minute, then pour it into the French press (preferably filling to capacity). The temperature of the steeping water should be from 195 to 205°F. There are two ways of doing this. You can start by pouring just enough water into the French press to cover the grounds and stir gently to create an initial rich foam, particularly if the coffee has been freshly ground. Then add the rest of the water. Alternatively, you can pour in all the water at once.

Stir gently, preferably with a plastic or wooden spoon so as to not crack the glass container, then place the top back onto the top of the coffeemaker with the filter screen in the fully raised position. Let the coffee gently steep for three to four minutes. Bear in mind that it takes a bit longer to extract larger coffee particles. Don't exceed four minutes or you will start extracting some of the bitter components. You may have to experiment a bit with different coffees and grinds. Lift off the top and stir once more just before replacing the plunger and compressing it.

Press the filter down firmly but gently. Some people cover the plunger screen with a thin paper basket filter to reduce the possibility of any grounds ending up in the finished coffee, but this makes the plunger a little more difficult to press. This will take away some of the flavor, but some people absolutely hate a mouthful of grounds—even fine ones.

Decant the coffee slowly into your cup to minimize the possibilities of including fine sediment particles. If you are not going to drink it all right away, don't let the coffee sit in the press after the brewing is finished. If you do, it will become bitter. Pour all the coffee into a glass container so you can gently reheat it in the microwave later or pour it into a thermos to keep it warm.

FILTER DRIP COFFEE

Because good filter coffeemakers are found everywhere, we have a tendency to take them for granted. Most people believe that they were invented either by the Melitta or Mr. Coffee companies. Although these famous names played pivotal roles in the development of the coffeemakers we see today, the history of drip coffee goes back a lot further.

Some believe that the first attempt to make a filtered coffee took place around 1710 in France, the result of someone putting coffee into a clean linen bag or wool sock then pouring boiling water over it to steep. It was called the infusion process, and tea was made in the same way. The coffee steeped or "infused" until the required strength was reached. In fact, this may be a true story because it appears to be simple enough. However, this method of making coffee did not appear to be popular.

The two countries claiming to invent the first filter coffeemakers are France and India. France should not be that much of a surprise because innumerable food and beverage advancements have come from there. On the other hand, India is somewhat surprising because most of us identify tea as the national beverage of choice and are thus a bit surprised that filtered coffee would have originated there.

In the case of France, the first drip coffeemaker was produced by a Monsieur Biggin in 1802. This was a cof-feepot with a long spout and a top that housed a can-like container with holes in its bottom and a water diffuser at its top. Coffee was simply placed into the can atop the pot and freshly boiled water was poured over the diffuser. The water dripped down through the grounds and extracted the coffee. As a result of gravity, the coffee continued to flow down through the holes in the bottom of the can and into the pot. This simple process is largely re-created in today's modern drip coffeemakers.

Drip coffee making in India began in the early 1800s and also used a can or cuplike receptacle with holes in the bottom to hold back the grounds. The coffee, however, was prepared in a different way. Fresh coffee grounds were spread lightly into the porous upper cup and compressed gently with a stemmed tamper containing holes. Boiling water was then poured on top of the compressed grounds while leaving the porous tamper in place. The extracted coffee dripped into the receiving receptacle at the bottom of the cup within a couple of hours and was ready for consumption.

Both methods are similar to one another in that gravity is used to pull the extraction water through the bed of grounds. Because the perforations were fairly large, it was not uncommon to see a considerable amount of sediment in the coffee. The first major improvement on this method came from the techniques of filtration routinely used in every laboratory—the use of a paper filter.

Melitta Bentz was a housewife from Dresden, that historic center of art and culture situated in a valley on the river Elbe in the Germany state of Saxony. In 1908 she thought of using paper to filter out unwanted coffee residues. She punctured the bottom of a brass pot and lined it with a piece of blotting paper that she had taken from her eldest son's school notebook. The result was a highly filtered coffee without any grounds or harshness. This form of coffee particularly suited the German consumers' taste with a clear preference for lighter-bodied beverages, as typified by their tradition of highly filtered wines.

Mrs. Bentz registered her invention with the patent office in Berlin and received confirmation on July 8, 1908. The title of her invention was "Filter Top Device lined with Filter Paper." The thirty-five-year-old made a quick conversion from housewife to entrepreneur and established a company bearing her name. During the 1930s the receiving top was changed to a cone-shape device, resulting in a greater surface area for the grounds. This improved the level of coffee extraction. A round filter paper was folded first in half then in half again, resulting in a conical shape to fit the filter. Shortly thereafter a patent was granted for a cone-shaped filter paper to fit inside the filter top. Additional developments were made over the years to electrify the filter drip coffeemaker and to improve the paper so as to allow more of the coffee's aroma and flavor to come through in the final cup.

Without any doubt, this is one of the most convenient ways of making good coffee and is a breeze to clean up.

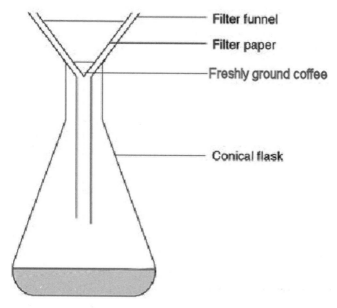

Laboratory coffee. (© Morton Satin, 2008.)

Of course, any graduate student with access to a "wet" laboratory is likely to have made his own form of filter coffee using a simple glass funnel, ground coffee, a filter paper, a glass beaker or flask (or cup for those "snotty types"), and a kettle of boiling water. A very successful variant of the filter drip coffeemaker was invented by Vincent Marotta, one of the many Italians who have dominated the history of coffee.

Marotta was the son of immigrants who worked in an Ohio coal mining business. Highly athletic, he signed a contract with the St. Louis Cardinals after graduating high school but decided to first attend college before devoting his career to sports. World War II broke out and immediately after his freshman year of college, he was drafted. Following his service in the armed forces, he returned to college, where he excelled in football. When he graduated, Marotta played professional football for a short time with the Cleveland Browns, his hometown team. After he left football, Marotta decided to get into construction and land development.

Marotta was very successful and by 1968 had become a leader in Cleveland's construction business. At the same time, Marotta wanted to design a better way to make coffee at home. Together with engineers Edward Able and Erwin Schulze, Marotta developed the Mr. Coffee machine in 1971. Because of its speed and convenience, the machine quickly became a best seller. By April 1974 more than 1 million Mr. Coffees had been sold. It remains the world's best-selling coffeemaker for domestic use.

With the millions of drip filter coffeemakers out there, each with its own instruction book, one would think there was really nothing else to add to the preparation of good drip filter coffee. Just to make sure you're using your coffeemaker to the best of its ability, there are a few basics to bear in mind.

First of all, start off with a decent quality of coffee with a medium to dark roast. Make sure that you have set the grind for drip filter. Freshly ground coffee makes an immense difference in your cup's final taste. Check the pot after you've finished with it to see if any fine grounds have come through. If they haven't, you might want to consider a slightly finer grind. The idea is to make sure that your whole system is integrated and that the coffee you choose is perfectly suited for the filter paper you use. Once you see residue in the bottom of the finished pot, you know the coffee has been ground too finely. Up until that point, the finer the coffee grind you can get away with, the greater the extraction rate will be.

Remember that coffee oils go rancid quickly, so make every effort to keep the entire coffeemaker as clean as possible. If the pot and the filter are dishwasher safe, put them in the dishwasher so that all vestiges of old coffee oil are removed.

It is important to the use fresh, cold water—not distilled water. It may be surprising to learn that distilled water is very corrosive because as many minerals as possible are scavenged and filtered out. It also makes for very flat coffee. On the other hand, make sure the water you are using is not too hard. If it is, use a softening filter such as those that routinely come with refrigerators.

It is not a good idea to use the brew pause feature, because you are interrupting the complete brewing cycle. You will inevitably have a "stronger than usual" cup.

When you replace the pot and continue the brewing process, the result will be "weaker than usual" for others sharing the pot.

Coffee cannot retain its flavor when it is kept hot, so avoid using the "keep warm" feature. You are much better off letting the coffee cool then carefully reheating it in the microwave (not to the boiling point).

Other than that, there is not much to it.

VACUUM COFFEE

Without doubt, the most elegant and fascinating way to make coffee is the vacuum method. Beginning in the first half of the nineteenth century, the idea evolved of heating water in a lower vessel until the heat of expansion forced the hot water through a narrow tube into an upper vessel that contained ground coffee. Once the lower vessel was empty and extraction of the coffee in the upper vessel was complete, the heat was removed and the resulting vacuum would draw the brewed coffee back through a strainer into the lower chamber, from which it could be served.

Because we are dealing with only the heat of expansion under normal atmospheric pressure, it was possible to work with glass and design various beautiful shapes of vessels through which one could see the outward movement of water and the return of finished coffee. The arti-

A vacuum coffeemarker. (© Morton Satin, 2008.)

sanship of the glassblower and perhaps even a metal artist working in copper or brass would result in a work of art as well as a coffee-making appliance.

The vacuum coffeepot underwent a number of design modifications in Europe, including a version called the "balancing siphon," which had the added feature of turning off the heater once the coffee was brewed.

The vacuum brewer was being used in the United States by the mid-nineteenth century but fell out of favor for a time. When the vacuum coffeemaker was reintroduced at the beginning of the twentieth century, it took on a distinctly American identity.

In 1915 a vacuum coffeemaker was introduced that was made from Corning Glass's new Pyrex heatproof glass. It was called a Silex coffeemaker, the name an acronym apparently derived from the phrase "Sanitary and Interesting method of making Luscious coffee. It is Easy to operate on account of its being X-ray transparent."[2] The acronym was a lot easier to remember than the functional description from which it was derived. Because the material was Pyrex, there was very little breakage associated with the product, so it soon became a standard device in hotels, restaurants, and catering establishments. It became so popular that even after many other companies started producing a similar product, everyone referred to the machines as Silex coffeepots. One of the most popular versions of this type of coffeemaker was produced by Sunbeam. On page 275 is

rom Page 25)

eye, he saw his funeral. A funeral people would talk about: a funeral that would give him importance after he was dead; however brief, a kind of immortality. Inarticulately, he longed for that, he longed for his name to be remembered a moment on earth.

But the real longing was deeper than that. It was racial; it was the feeling that after the oppressions and the subservience and the compromises of a black man's life, he had a right, it was fitting, it was his due, to enjoy, in death, a moment of supreme importance before his dust went unto dust, William, at the thought of that moment, smiled.

"I got mo' what friends 'n any two men," he said, "I gwan have one jam-up buryin'."

"You got de friends," Lucindy said. "And you got, too, a impty belly and wuk to do and a mo'gage on de home. You got plenty to fret wid, 'thout frettin' 'bout yo' fun'al."

William's smile left his face, and it was with weariness that he climbed the two steps to the gallery, Lucindy following, and sank down in the rocking chair.

"Lucindy, take off my boots."

Lucindy looked at him.

"You's tired," she said. She got down on her knees and removed his gaiters. "You's all jaded out."

William put his head back, folded his hands in his lap, and in three minutes was snoring mightily.

At sundown Lucindy wakened him. "Supper's on de table," In silence they ate the grits and pork and turnip greens; Lucindy placid, William frowning, thinking.

He was thinking that he was old, that he would die before long. Death, until the last few days a distant and not particularly unpleasant prospect, had quietened, after the talk in the shop and Mr. Harper's funeral, become close.

There were things he had intended doing before he died. He had thought he had plenty of time for them. Now ——

He sat at the table with his shoulders bent down, feeling the mortgage—a matter of four hundred dollars—a palpable thing over the house, like a blanket. It was somehow as if the mortgage itself were the roof.

Lucindy had been a good woman for him. For a long time she had fed him and mended his clothes. She had never been mean. She had been just right, just exactly. It seemed to William that the least he could do ——

He walked to work the next morning bemused, thinking hard. And when General Fragonard came in for his trim, and sat down and started reading the morning Statesman, William spoke: 'Fine mawnin', suh."

"Fine," General Fragonard said.

"Meks a man feel young agin."

"Like a colt," General Fragonard said.

"Sho puts skittishness in de old rore-out bones."

General Fragonard nodded.

"Meks de stove-up old bones 'n' moos lak new, suh."

"I'm."

"Fo' de flittin' moment," William said profoundly.

General Fragonard's eyes rolled toward the impassive black face. "You,

Sunbeam coffee ad.

a 1950s ad for the coffeemaker and the photograph of the same model, which I purchased on eBay at a very reasonable price.

The key to making good vacuum-brewed coffee is the size of the grind (which should be similar to that of filter coffee but on the coarser end), the temperature of the water when it mixes with the coffee, and the time of the brewing. By the end of the 1950s, these coffeemakers dropped in popularity to be replaced by the beast of all coffeemakers—the percolator.

These days, vacuum coffeemakers are coming back into vogue because they make good coffee and because people like their elegant look. For those who enjoy nostalgia, they can still find the older styles, in perfectly good shape, on eBay.

PERCOLATED COFFEE

James H. Mason patented the first coffee percolator in the United States on December 26, 1865. In a sense, the percolator acts like a combination vacuum/drip coffeemaker. The water in the pot is heated and rises up through a central tube, eventually spilling over onto a metal basket holding the coffee grounds—that is, the vacuum part. After the water infuses the coffee grounds in the basket, it filters its way back down through the bottom holes in the basket. The coffee then continues to cycle until it reaches the desired strength. All too often, this continual reheating and recycling of the coffee through the grounds makes the brew bitter.

As with all coffee making, you need to make sure all the equipment is clean. This is particularly true for a percolator because it extracts a lot of coffee oils. It is best to use a milder coffee such as a Colombian blend with a light to medium roast. The grind should be medium to coarse, but not as coarse as that for a French press. Whether or not you use electricity as the heat source, start with cold, good-tasting water. Once finished with its five-minute cycle, never reboil the coffee.

ESPRESSO

My family and I were fortunate enough to live in Italy for close to twenty years. Whenever I want to relax, I simply close my eyes and some vision of my Italian paradise comes into view. Sometimes it is the beach at Sperlonga (halfway between Rome and Naples), another time it's the Gargano Peninsula overlooking the Adriatic, or peering down into a Tuscan valley from the top of Montalcino, or the Arco Naturale in Capri, or the Gonzaga palace in Mantua, or . . .

Of course it's never just the locations, but also the people. I have always found it a terrible pity that so many occasional visitors did not get to know the people better, but that is another story. And of course it's not just the place and the people, but in every happy reverie, there is the food, the glorious food. When it comes to food or drink, Italians know what they are doing—period, end of story.

One way or another, I have been in the food business for all my life. From the age of twelve, during the summers I worked in snack bars, restaurants, and private dining clubs until I left graduate school, so I had learned how to cook. I am critical of cooking and am seldom impressed with décor, pretense, or cuisine condescension. But I do love good food and drink—perfect blends of flavors, striking textures, heavenly aromas, and arresting presentations. In the almost twenty years we lived in Italy, we never had a bad meal.

During the summer months, on most Sundays I drove up to Porto Ercole on the Argentario Peninsula to go scuba diving in the Tyrrhenian Sea. One of the advantages of doing a lot of field work for the United Nations is that you get to travel. I was director of the Global Agro-industries Development program. Everywhere I went that had a sea nearby, I brought along my diving gear. When going out for a day of diving, most people bring along a sandwich or two for lunch. Not in Italy. The first time I took a boat off of Porto Ercole, I went into my knapsack and fished out a sandwich at lunchtime. I was about to take a bite when I heard the captain yell at me, "Morton, *cosa stai facendo?*" *What are you doing?* I answered, "*Ho un panino.*" *I have a sandwich*. The captain looked at me with a great deal of pity and said, "*Ma abbiamo la pasta!*" *But we have pasta!* I got up and looked into his little cabin and there was a big pot of pasta cooking. My sandwiches ended up feeding the fish and I enjoyed a terrific *penne arrabiata*, followed by an excellent caffè straight out of a beat-up old expresso machine.

Italians are a dynamic people. They talk quickly and gesticulate animatedly. The first time you take a drive on the *autostrada*, you will discover their love for speed. Time is always of the essence—things must be done quickly. Why? So you can have time to relax! What a silly question!

It's no wonder that the espresso machine was developed in Italy. Espresso means fast. How can one simply stand around and wait for coffee? The whole purpose for the most brilliant idea in coffee-making history derived from nothing more than simple impatience. Compulsion was the mother of invention.

The modern espresso maker should not be considered a simple feat of engineering. Its innovators had goals in common with rocket scientists: both had to defy gravity. The time it took water to pass through and extract coffee grounds from a filter coffeemaker was controlled by gravity. Of course, vacuum coffeemakers had the assistance of a partial vacuum to help speed the passage through the grounds, but it took so long for a vacuum machine to heat up and cleaning it took forever.

Something better had to be developed to make good coffee in less time.

The idea of using steam pressure to extract coffee developed during the nineteenth century, but the first practical espresso machine was developed just at the turn of the century. In 1901 Luigi Bezzera of Milan patented a machine that not only produced coffee quickly but also an extremely high-quality beverage. His coffee machine was based on using steam from a gas-heated brass boiler. It forced heated water through a filter basket of coffee grounds directly into a cup. This newly designed filter, called a head or a "group," was designed to withstand a pressure of about 1.5 atmospheres, the equivalent of 22 pounds per square inch. By opening a knob, first water then steam passed through the ground coffee in the filter. This enabled the brewing of coffee to take place in just one minute. The machine was also fitted with hot water and steam pipes to prepare hot drinks.

Each charge of fresh coffee grounds ended up as a custom-made coffee expressly for the customer. Hence the name *espresso*. Water was *expressed* through the coffee *expressly* for one customer in an *express* time—a triple play on words. No matter if someone wanted his coffee a touch more diluted (*lunghetto*) or a bit more diluted than that (*lungo*), or if someone else wanted it with less water and more concentrated (*ristretto*), each one could be individually tailored by the operator. The coffee wasn't perfect, but it was a start.

In 1903 Bezzera sold his patent to Desiderio Pavoni, who ran a little workshop at Via Parini in Milan. In 1905 Pavoni started to manufacture and sell espresso machines and was immediately followed by Victoria Arduino from Turin. Few changes in design were made to the mechanics of the machine. However, its popularity remained limited because of the occasional burnt taste that resulted from the exposure of the grounds directly to the steam when the operator was not watching.

Achille Gaggia was the proprietor of a pastry shop in Milan and was always on the lookout for new coffeemakers. In 1938 he purchased from the widow of an inventor named Cremonesi a patent for a new machine that forced water through the coffee by means of a piston. The advantage of this machine was that its piston pump forced hot—but not boiling—water through the coffee, so it was never burnt. He put the machine in his pastry shop but was unable to use it because of the outbreak of World War II.

In 1948, after the war had ended, Gaggia changed the world of coffee forever with a new machine called the Classica that totally eliminated direct steam injection. At a temperature of precisely 92°C (197.6°F), water from a small boiler was forced through the coffee at approximately 9 atmospheres of pressure by means of a hand pump. The result was a revolution—an espresso that was capped by a characteristic head of foamy *crema*. The Gaggia machine was an instant success.

From that moment on, having a fine crema—that heavenly caramel-colored emulsion of essential coffee oils floating on the surface—has been the goal of all espresso makers.

Cappuccino was the simple extension of espresso coffee to which steamed milk was added. Baristas found that when milk was properly steamed, a marvelously thick, rich foam collected at the top of the coffee. So with time, the modern-day cappuccino was born. The history of the word *cappuccino* demonstrates how words can evolve as they are integrated into a lexicon. The Capuchin monks took their Italian name from the long, pointed cowl, or cappuccino hood, that was worn as part of the order's habit. The name of this order was later used as the name of a small monkey with a tuft of black, cowl-like hair. In Italian, cappuccino went on to mean an "espresso coffee mixed or topped with steamed milk," so that the color of the coffee resembled the color of a Capuchin monk's habit.

The first thing you need for making espresso is a good espresso maker. When buying a machine, keep a couple of things in mind. First of all, understand that you can spend anywhere from fifty to five thousand dollars or more for a single home espresso maker. They all make espresso. There are differences in the quality of construction, engineering, and aesthetics. If your main interest is making coffee, focus on the construction and the engineering. This has the tendency of eliminating the

A fast and practical espresso machine. (© Morton Satin, 2008.)

lower-priced machines. Have a look at the quality of the coffee baskets, the knobs, and the switches and you will immediately be able to tell if there is a certain machine you want to invest in. It is difficult to get a decent quality machine for less than two hundred dollars.

Then there are machines, some of which are completely handmade, that will cost you almost the price of a small car. Some of these are superbly made, beautiful to behold, and are no doubt conversation pieces. But, in the hands of a good barista, any solid, well-designed espresso machine will do a fine job. Most important, there isn't a five-thousand-dollar espresso machine anywhere that will make better coffee than a four-hundred-dollar one if the quality and grind of the coffee going in is not just right. Each espresso machine comes with its own instructions, so I will add only a few additional comments.

When you make espresso, you should be using filtered water from a home filtration system, a countertop water filter, a refrigerator filter, or a Brita water filter. (In many locations in Italy, the water is very hard and all the commercial espresso makers have built-in water conditioners that require a saltwater back flush every morning to recharge the ion-exchange resins. You have to make sure you're not the first customer of the morning or else your coffee will be salty.) Make sure you de-scale your machine every two to three months. If you keep the water in the reservoir for long periods without using it,

A portafilter with coffee. (© Morton Satin, 2008.)

there may be a possibility of algae development. If you are concerned about this, buy a little waterproof UV water pen from an aquarium shop and turn it on for thirty minutes once a week to keep algae from blooming. If you change the water at least once a week, there is no need for this. But it is a good idea to clean out everything at least once a month.

The most important part of any espresso is the quality and the grind of coffee. Bear in mind that the term quality has a subjective element to it, depending on an individual's taste. The one thing about quality that no one can argue about is its reliability. Whatever it is today,

A beautiful blend of beans. (© Morton Satin, 2008.)

it should be tomorrow and next week, so that there are no surprises. Consistency is a central element of quality. After that, it is very much up to the drinker.

I have seen Italian roasters do wonders with blends containing less expensive robusta beans in addition to arabica, but I was witnessing the result of generations of passed-down experience. If the ability is not there to manipulate a poor-quality coffee to bring out its very best attributes, then the higher-quality blends of pure arabica beans are a must. Notice that I referred to a blend of beans rather than a single source. It's a bit like the difference between single-malt and blended whiskeys: single-source coffees play up to a person's pretensions because they are special, but blends are what people drink because they are delicious.

The coffee beans should be roasted on the dark side, but not charred black. A medium-dark roast is probably the most suitable. There has to be a certain sensitivity to the delicate nature of the beans, and roasting shouldn't be overdone to a point where nuances are obliterated by an overwhelming strong, acidic flavor. That is not to say that the flavor of a good espresso is a shrinking violet—on the contrary, the flavor should be rich, powerful, and balanced. I have had marvelous results with AA Kenya beans blended with some Jamaican Blue Mountain, but there are many that will do equally well or even better. Have a bit of confidence in your own taste, and experiment until you find a coffee that perfectly suits you.

Of course, the next most important thing is the grinder, which should be adjusted for the specific characteristics of your machine. Espresso grind is always fine, but nowhere near as fine as a Turkish grind. The problem is that each machine has its own idiosyncrasies and your coffee grinder has to be adjusted to it. To make matters more complicated, even if you have the best grinder and it is kept at one setting, the variability in size of the grinds will differ depending upon the type of coffee you use. Even the amount of time since it was roasted and the level of humidity will have an impact on the size of the final grind.

Tamping down the coffee. (© Morton Satin, 2008.)

When the water hits the coffee and starts to perfuse it, a back pressure has to build in order to force the water and the oil/water emulsion through the grinds. If the coffee is too coarse, the hot water will quickly run through without a back pressure ever being built. If the coffee is ground too fine, you'll get a great deal of back pressure but the water will never flow through the compact mass of grinds. You have to get a just right grind so that the water drips through slowly and you end up with an espresso in twenty-five to thirty seconds.

Once the portafilter is filled and the coffee has been tamped down, twist the filter into the group head as far as it will go. In order to get a bit of extra back pressure, some people prefer to pump water through for only a second then stop and further tighten the portafilter a bit. Then they finish making their espresso in the normal way. This should only be done with larger, more robust machines costing five hundred dollars or more, as the extra pressure may damage the pumps of smaller machines.

You have to listen to your coffee as it's being brewed. The sound of the pump will change in the last few seconds when the crema starts coming out. It's as if the machine knows it has done its job and is starting to relax. I don't like doing a lot of work every morning, so I grind my coffee beans only once a week. I know it would be better if they were freshly ground each day, but we all make sacrifices.

I usually have cappuccino at breakfast and my preference for a midmorning and after-lunch coffee is a *lungo macchiato*, which contains a bit more water than in a normal espresso and is topped up by a dollop of dense milk foam. It is like a tiny, ultra-rich cappuccino. (As mentioned earlier, the term *macchiato* comes from the Italian word *macchia*, or stain. It's black espresso "stained" with a touch of milk.)

Italians do wonderful things to coffee, and none is better than café correto, which is simply an espresso that has been "corrected." How? With a healthy shot of liquor, of course—grappa, brandy, or sambuca will do nicely, thank you—no need for macchiato.

The basis for any good cappuccino is a good espresso coffee to which foamed milk is added. The official Italian standard calls for a proportion of ⅕ espresso, ⅘ steamed milk, but most people prefer ¼ espresso with ¾ milk. Producing the milk froth is not easy for two reasons: First, not all espresso machines are capable of making a decent froth. Second, the sort of froth that was served for years in the United States was totally wrong! Milk froth should not be light and fluffy like a bubble bath—all you end up with is a milk mustache and no taste! Perhaps froth is the wrong word. You have to make a dense foam—like the Tempur-Pedic Swedish mattress—dense, yet soft and rich.

First, fill a small jug with fresh milk a quarter to a third full. Insert the espresso machine steam wand just below the surface of the milk and turn on the steam, gradually lowering the jug so that the wand always stays just beneath the rising surface. Don't blast the milk out of the jug. The idea is to develop microcells so that the volume increases by only a third or so. Listen to the sound of the milk changing as it starts to thicken. Learn to check the temperature of the milk by hand and when you feel it is ready, turn off the steam and pour gently.

(You can get an idea of the right feel by placing a food-grade thermometer in the milk while it is steaming.) Bring the temperature to about 132°F. You can sprinkle a bit of chocolate powder over the top (the Italians call it *polvore di marmo*, or marble powder), but it is not necessary. That's it.

The most recent development in the art of making coffee is the coffee pod. The idea for coffee pods is not new. Just as tea bags represented the means to make a unique single serving through variations in the time of steeping or the amount of water used, by adjusting the grind of coffee and placing it into a diffusible bag or pod, a similar degree of individuality could be achieved. The first patent for espresso pods made with filter paper bags was issued in 1959, but it did not prove popular because the preponderance of espresso machines were in use by commercial coffee bars who liked to retain their ability to use the roast and grind of coffee of their own choosing and to exercise the art of coffee making as they saw fit. The one exception was for the use of decaffeinated coffee, where the volume required was too small to warrant custom roasting and a specific in-house grinder. Thus, it was common to see the use of decaffeinated coffee pods in the espresso machines in most coffee bars.

With the continued growth in coffee consumption and the interest of consumers in receiving individual treatment, the idea of using pod machines began to catch on and brewers were developed for the home market and food service establishments where espresso making was not a specialty. Pods eliminated the need for training while still allowing for individual servings.

The illy company in Italy created a standard format called the Easy Serving Espresso design in 1998 as a means of encouraging a wide adoption by other coffee makers while providing consumers confidence in the idea of pods. All these pods were designed to be used in espresso machines, and most coffee lovers considered the taste to be inferior to traditional espresso that was made with freshly ground beans. Nevertheless, the idea began to take hold.

Individual ground coffee in plastic capsules was a variation of the coffee pod idea. The main difference was that these new pods were not designed to be used in an espresso maker, but rather machines designed explicitly to accommodate the pods. The designs of the pods and their specific machines were not standardized, so there are now a great many options for consumers to choose from, including Senseo, Nespresso, and Tassimo.

One of the most popular designs also happens to be the simplest, the Keurig K-Cup. In this system, the foil seal on top of the plastic K-Cup is pierced and the coffee (or tea or cocoa) is brewed by a spray of water kept at a precise temperature. This system is not designed to brew under the pressures used in other pod-type or espresso machines; however, the machine designs allow for variations in water temperatures as well as the volume of water used to brew the coffee. Because of the popularity of the K-Cup system, many coffee manufacturers have availed themselves of the Keurig licensing, so there are now a great many varieties to choose from. Keurig machines for the home even have a reusable filter called the My-K Cup, which allows regular ground coffee of the owner's choosing to be used.

Coffee lovers have much to look forward to. The renaissance in coffee appreciation has spawned a flood of new designs, machines, and brands. Since there are no signs that this trend is slowing down, we can expect more new and creative developments in the art and science of making our favorite brew in the future.

Enjoy!

13

The Barista's Art

Professional baristas spend hours mastering the artistic and technical elements of making the perfect-tasting and perfect-looking cappuccino or latte. There is even the World Barista Championship at which rival baristas from around the globe come to display their artistic abilities.

Just as food is treated with great respect in Italy, those who serve food and beverages are treated likewise. Being a server or a barista is not considered a second-rate job. The employees are considered integral parts of the establishment, which is why they generally stay for life. They are paid a good salary and are not dependent on gratuities.

Like any good bartender, the Italian barista specializes in understanding his clients. That is not to say that he or she is there to hold hands while someone is crying in his beer; most baristas are too busy to do so. In the very short period that an average customer is at the bar (two to three minutes at most), the barista has to learn and remember how each one likes his coffee. Does the client want a really strong shot of coffee? Then he needs a *ristretto*, meaning the water is restricted. The less the water, the thicker and more concentrated the coffee. It should all go down in one quick sip.

Others like to take the time to spread their coffee over several sips. So, the espresso could be *normale*, *lungo*, *lungetto*, or even *lungissimo*, each one adding a bit more water until you come to the final stop, beyond which no barman will ever venture—*Americano*, which reflects the amount of water in a typical American-style coffee.

The same can be said for the addition of the steamed milk, *macchia*, or stain. Most people will take *macchia caldo* (steamed milk), but some prefer *macchia fredo* (cold milk). If you like a lot of milk, you simply say *macchiatissimo* and the barista will understand.

I recall one day in the spring of 1991 when I took a Canadian friend to a bar in the Castelli Romano, the hills or "castles" just to the south of Rome. It was Sunday and we drove up to have a midmorning coffee and enjoy the beautiful view of Rome from the bar's terrace. As we walked up to the bar, an old fellow who was standing there told the barista, "*Café correto*." My friend looked at me quizzically, so I leaned over and whispered to him, "That's an espresso, with a shot of liquor in it." The barista prepared an espresso, then opened a bottle of Grand Marnier and proceeded to fill the old fellow's cup up to the brim. My friend's eyes opened wide in disbelief. "How much is he going to charge for that?" he gasped to me. "Two dollars—one for the espresso and one for the correto," I answered. "But that's impossible," my friend responded. "There are about two ounces of Grand Marnier in there!" I smiled knowingly and responded, "I'll tell you what, why don't we ask the barman how he can make a profit on that transaction."

We waited till the old man left the bar and I leaned over and asked the barista, "How is it possible for you to make a profit when you poured so much liquor into that man's café correto?" He continued to wipe down his counter and said, "Some people like more liquor and some like less. It all averages out. That man is over eighty-five years old and without a good shot of liquor, he would barely make it through the day. Besides, he is my client." He turned around and tended to other chores.

Relating to the customer is what it's all about. When my wife and I dropped by our local bar for a cappuccino, the barista would inevitably make a beautiful design on the surface of my wife's cup—not mine, only my wife's. One day, I furled my eyebrow and asked him, "How come my wife gets a beautiful design on her cappuccino and I don't?" He slightly lowered his head and looked at me over the top rim of his glasses and said, "When you come into my bar wearing a dress, I'll make you a fancy cappuccino."

I'm not certain when or where the idea of creating designs on the surface of the cappuccino came from. Making a heart or a spade is not particularly difficult when you have a practiced hand. It is one way for a barista to show his attention and respect for the ladies. For some, gender doesn't matter, they just want to show the client that they are paying attention to him or her. The standard tip that one leaves an Italian barista is something around a hundred lire, or ten cents (now 0.10)—certainly nothing to make a special effort over. The effort is made regardless of any possible gratuity. It is simply made because he is *your* barista.

But the life of a barista doesn't revolve around latte art. They are very hardworking. They open early and work long hours. The equipment has to be running in tip-top order at the start of the day and generally they throw out the first half dozen cups of coffee. This is because the machines have built-in water conditioners to cut down on the water hardness that is so common in Italy, so they have to perform a daily back flush with salt water to regenerate the ion-exchange resins. This causes the first few cups to be salty. They also like to make sure that the portafilter is coated with a layer of good coffee before they start serving.

A busy bar can serve thousands in a day during which time the barista has to stand on his feet, be cheerful, and carry on civil conversation (including comments on the football scores). He does all this while repeatedly churning out high-quality coffee. On a bad day, such as the day after a favorite team lost a home game, baristas are expected to be in a particularly foul mood—as are all his customers. This is usually shown by treating all the customers roughly and wearing a scowl throughout the day. I've seen baristas who were normally as close as brothers almost come to blows in front of customers to show how upset they were. Of course, this is highly appreciated by customers who also are in a terrible mood.

On top of that, they usually have to take care of the lunchtime sandwiches, the panini and tremazzini, ensuring that they are always covered with a damp cloth to keep them fresh. The thousands of cups and dishes have to be washed and all the supplies replenished. It takes a special person to have the patience to make a fancy cappuccino at four in the afternoon after having already served fifteen hundred coffees that same day. But being a barista is a serious job that is held in high respect by all Italians.

It did not take long before the idea of latte art—those little images that the barista forms on the surface of your cappuccino when pouring the steamed milk—caught on. That bit of extra attention that the barista took in serving your coffee became a challenge to up-and-coming baristas in other countries. It was not long before adding that little something extra turned competitive.

In 2000, Alf Kramer, the first president of the Specialty Coffee Association of Europe, arranged to develop a world competition for baristas. The idea was based on the barista competitions previously held in Norway. It would be an opportunity to show off the talents of competitive baristas from all over the world at the World Barista Championship (WBC). At the same time that it could bring much greater attention to the specialty coffee industry, it might also motivate baristas to do more with coffee and would set a standard of service across the globe. No one can argue with the success of cooking competitions such as those on *Iron Chef*.

The first event was held in 2000 in Monte Carlo. Twelve individuals from around the world attended. The honor of the first competition went to Robert Thoresen of Norway, with second place going to Erla Kristisdottir of Iceland, and third place to Martin Hildebrandt of Denmark—a perfect Nordic hat trick. The Italian representative came in fifth.

The following year, the competition was moved across the pond to Miami, despite the hot and steamy weather. The number of competitors jumped to seventeen. The first place went to Martin Hildebrandt of Denmark, second place to Tim Wendelboe of Norway, and third place to Roberto dell Aquilla of Sweden—another perfect Nordic hat trick. The Italian representative came in fifth, again.

After two Nordic hat tricks in a row, there was no way the baristas from other parts of the world would allow this to be repeated, even though the 2002 annual World Barista Championship was scheduled to take place in Oslo, Norway. The competition was growing, and twenty-four baristas from around the world joined in the fight for the coveted title. Improbable as it may sound, first place went to Fritz Storm of Denmark and second place to Tim Wendelboe of Norway. However, the Nordics would no longer have a sweep. They were denied third place. That honor was given to . . . Vikram Kurana of India. India? Of course, we all know that coffee came to India long before it came to Europe, but an Indian barista champion? Absolutely! The Italian representative moved up to fourth place.

In Boston in 2003, first place went to Paul Bassett of Australia, second place to Asa Petterson of Iceland, and third place to Eirik Johnsen of Norway. Italy came in ninth out of twenty-four representatives. Even when the competition moved to Trieste, Italy, in 2004, the amazing Tim Wendleboe of Norway came in first, Sammy Piccolo of Canada came in second, and Klaus Thomsen of Denmark, third. Italy dropped down to twenty-sixth out of thirty-four. And so it went.

Why was it that Italy, the spiritual domain of the barista, never won a competition? Was there something particular about the World Barista Championship that did not appeal to the Italian nature? Could it be the rigidity of the rules, because that is something that seems to rankle the Italian character. Let's look at them.

We can start with the WBC definition of espresso.

1. An espresso is one ounce/30 ml liquid including crema, ±5 ml is allowed.
2. Each single espresso should be produced with an appropriate and consistent amount of ground coffee.
3. Espresso shall be brewed at a temperature between 195–205 degrees Fahrenheit / 90.5–96 degrees Celsius.
4. Machine brewing pressure will be 8.5 to 9.5 atmospheres.
5. Extraction time must be between 20 to 30 seconds.
6. Espressos must be served in a 2 to 3 ounce / 60 to 90 ml cup with a handle.
7. Espressos should be served to the judges immediately complete with spoon, napkin, sugar and water.

That's a bit rigid because those things that a barista can control are the things that make a coffee unique for the particular client. What about a WBC cappuccino?

1. Cappuccino is a beverage of ratios, producing a harmonious balance of one (1) single shot of espresso, steamed milk, and frothed milk.
2. A traditional cappuccino is a 5 to 6 ounce / 150 to 180 ml beverage.
3. A cappuccino should be served in a 5 to 6 ounce / 150 to 180 ml cup with a handle.
4. Any additional toppings, spices or powdered flavorings are not allowed.[1]

Although many prefer a cup, some love their cappuccino in a glass. In fact, the whole idea of rigid standards for an espresso and a cappuccino seem a bit contrary to the basic concept. An espresso is made *expressly* for someone. Standardizing the product and its presentation just seems so contrary to what a barista normally does—though, of course, every competition must have some basic governing rules, so they are not likely to change too quickly.

There is absolutely no doubt that the creations these champions made were quite phenomenal. The ability to form such beautiful patterns on the surface of a cup of cappuccino is very impressive and the fact that someone gets to enjoy the wonderful taste of such a creation makes it all the more fantastic. I'm quite certain that most of the baristas in Italy would take great pleasure in watching the experts at the World Barista Championship do their thing. To a certain extent, I'm sure they could relate to these competitors, but, on the other hand, that is not their real job. Their real job is to establish and maintain a relationship with their clients. They can certainly indulge in some latte art, but what is presented at the WBC may be considered *un po 'di un'esagerazione*— a bit of an exaggeration.

Tim Wendelboe, that amazing Norwegian who came in first in the 2004 WBC and second in the 2002 and 2001 competitions, voiced his concern in an excellent article titled "The Future of the World Barista Championship," which appeared on the CoffeeGeek Web site taken from Viva Barista:

> What if a barista is able to pull the best espresso ever made on planet earth in a 19 second extraction? He/she will loose 1 point per judge because of the required 20 to 30 second extraction time. Does this mean that he/she has to compromise the espresso quality to be able to meet the WBC standards and have a chance to become the world champion? The answer is definitely, yes.[2]

I am very grateful for the existence of the World Barista Championship and hope it continues to grow and become more popular. It is a marvel to see these experts at work. They do a lot for the industry and they fascinate consumers such as myself. It may not necessarily showcase the talents of my favorite barista, but it sets an example of what can be created if one is determined, disciplined, and talented.

As I said, my personal barista has other priorities. I recall when I first entered his bar on Viale Aventino in Rome, he didn't give me a second look. The coffee was good, but I was nobody and was treated as such. After continuing to come to his bar on a daily basis, it didn't take more than two weeks or so before he began smiling at me in recognition. From that point on, I made sure to compliment him on the quality of his coffee.

After about six months, I dropped by toward the end of the lunch period and asked for my coffee. He hesitated for a moment, took out a cappuccino-size cup, and pulled an espresso for me. As he handed me the cup, I quizzically asked if he'd run out of espresso cups. "Taste it," he said. I took a sip and it seemed even better than usual. "It's great!" I said, "How did you do it?" "It's the cup," he said with a knowing wink. "When you bring it up, your nose gets to smell the aroma much better in a large cup."

I congratulated him once again and told him how great it was. He leaned over conspiratorially, held a finger to his lips, and whispered, "Signor Satin, you're the only foreigner that I tell this, because I know how much you like coffee." With that, I walked out of the bar feeling like one of the most privileged people in the world.

14

Espressilogue

When we started this voyage, I recounted some of the ways in which coffee has had an impact on my life. Of course, my appreciation of coffee was greatly enriched by the opportunity my family had to live in Italy for almost two decades. Italy is the spiritual home of modern coffee culture. The espresso technology, originally developed at the beginning of the twentieth century, remains the pinnacle of coffee brewing for most people. Even though many will not go through the trouble of making a proper espresso at home, they greatly appreciate it from their local coffee bar or when they travel abroad.

If you examine the modern interest in coffee, you will hear much discussion of different beans, locales, and cupping tests. You will even hear talk of the French press being the purest way to produce coffee, but given the taste of most people, espresso-based coffees are what everyone wants. In fact, sales of espresso machines have never been higher. No longer satisfied with the lower end of the product line, some people are choosing to spend thousands of dollars for home espresso makers and up to a thousand dollars for a coffee grinder. I am not referring to Middle Eastern oil sheiks or Hollywood stars, but everyday individuals who have developed an absolute passion for coffee and are willing to give up many other things in their lives in order to indulge it, whether they live in Minneapolis, Rio de Janeiro, Bangalore, or Shanghai.

Italy continues to influence the tastes of the rest of the world. For centuries, the rest of Europe looked across the Alps with envy to the cultural and environmental splendor there. Not a poet, artist, member of the landed gentry, or any young person for that matter would think of a grand tour of Europe without having Italy as the ultimate destination. The glory of Italian art, music, opera, architecture, technological genius, and of course, its food and wine, have been the envy of Europe and of the world. Because it is such a conservative country, it has held on to all its traditions, the most important being *la bella figura*.

Literally translated, *la bella figura* means *a good face*, pertaining to the emphasis of maintaining a proper and honorable image. That is the reason why quality is so highly valued in this country. It would not be good for one's image if he made something cheap—it would be *bruta figura*, or *ugly face*. At all costs one must avoid a bruta figura because it not only reflects on the individual but also his or her family—and nothing is more important than family honor in that country. *Family values* is not merely a slogan there.

Perhaps the phenomenon of la bella figura has entrenched itself into today's coffee renaissance. The devotion to high quality—be it in the beans, the way they are roasted, the machinery to grind them or to brew espresso, or even the presentation techniques—is essential for coffee keeping its bella figure. Therefore, I thought it fitting to end *Coffee Talk* with some recollections as a *straniero*, or foreigner, of how important coffee is to Italians.

Every Sunday morning, our family and friends would meet at the coffee bar. We would patiently wait for a couple of the *al fresco* tables to become available and would take a seat while the chosen ones would go in and order cappuccinos or lattés for the kids. Of course, the drinks would always be accompanied by a big plate of cornettos or other pastries. On Sundays, the baristas were at their best, decorating the beverages with various designs and always placing a delicious little wrapped chocolate on each plate, beside the coffee cups. We would then spend a lazy half hour or hour telling stories about our experiences in that remarkable country.

Here are a few of them.

THE STOP SIGN

The second year my family and I were in Italy, we decided to drive down to Sicily to spend Christmas. After all, Sicily jutted out into the belly of the Mediterranean and we felt the weather would be a bit better than the cold and very damp winter climate in Rome. As an added bonus, we would be in Sicily for the beginning of the season for the wonderful blood oranges that our kids adored.

Since everyone cautioned me that my car would be hijacked and I'd have to pay a ransom to get it back, we decided to drive down to Sicily in a rental car. After picking up the rental and paying a hefty surcharge for the insurance, the family piled in and we got going, hoping to make the town of Taormina, just beside Mount Etna, by nightfall. Unfortunately that did not happen because the superb autostrada system deteriorates significantly just past Naples. Southern Italians have a distaste for paying taxes, and their roadway infrastructure reflects this. Whereas you could comfortably cruise at 160 to 200 kilometers per hour (100 to 125 miles per hour!) on the autostrada anywhere north of Naples, you have to slow down to 100 to 130 kph (60 to 80 mph) in the southern stretches or you'll end up a casualty. We eventually stopped at a decent roadside hotel the first night, still another two hours before we would cross the Straits of Messina to get onto the island of Sicily. We called ahead to a hotel in Taormina to make sure we would have a room the following night.

We started out early the next morning, entered the chaotic lineup for the ferry at Reggio Calabria, and entered Messina around noon. There, we found a small restaurant with a view of the port, relaxed for a leisurely lunch, then finished the easy drive to Taormina. We were extremely lucky because we had an excellent room with a superb little balcony looking straight out at Mount Etna. That night, we were thoroughly entertained by the constant eruptions of the active volcano. What a sight! The family hit the sack very pleased with what they had seen and with great expectations for the next day. Our eldest daughter was interested in Greek history, so we planned to visit the Greek amphitheater in Siracusa the next morning.

We got off to a comfortable start after a great breakfast of Sicilian pastries and cappuccino. Soon after getting back on the road, the highway ended and we were on a small state road. I had looked at the map and thought we might make an interesting little loop into the countryside before heading back toward Siracusa. We turned off at a town called Primosole (where the sun first rises on Sicily) and headed inland on a small road.

We turned a corner and I saw a stop sign that seemed to come out of nowhere. I jammed on the brakes and within a second a small car hit us from behind. Everyone was more shocked than hurt because we thought we were alone on the road. The middle-aged driver in the other car threw his door open and came toward me, yelling in Italian, "Why did you stop all of a sudden?" I turned for a second look at the stop sign. Then, pointing to the stop sign, I responded in my best Italian, "Because there is a stop sign here!"

The man rolled his eyes up, shook his head from side to side, held his hands out, fingers clenched upward, and said, "Idiot, no one ever stops at this stop sign!"

I was about to answer him when a small, dark blue Fiat rolled up and came to a stop behind us. The car was marked "Polizia." A very heavy and tall policeman in a Carabinieri uniform managed to squeeze out the front door. He straightened to his full height, patted down all the creases in his uniform, adjusted his cap firmly, and strode toward us with an air of seriousness.

"Excuse me, what has happened here?" he asked, his voice heavy with gravitas. The other fellow quickly gesticulated toward me, then tapped his skull a few times with his index finger and rapidly told the policeman that the idiot foreigner had stopped at a place where nobody else stops. The policeman looked at me, then at the other fellow, and quietly said, "*Patente*" (driver's license), and held out his hand to the other fellow and then to me. We both handed him our driver's licenses and the police officer immediately saw that I had diplomatic status in Italy. He clicked his heels, quietly asked me my version of the story, then looked with a jaundiced eye upon my perspiring antagonist.

The policeman shook his head and said to me in

Italian, "Do not preoccupy yourself, sir. It is obviously this man's fault for hitting you in the back. I will immediately give him a ticket for his bad driving, and send a copy to you to show your insurance company so that you will not have to pay anything. He will be totally responsible for this. It's clear that he is an imbecile. Look at him sweating that way—pity the poor man."

He walked back to the fellow and started to berate him while filling out a form that appeared to be a ticket. I looked at the back of my rental car and there didn't seem to be any damage whatsoever. The policeman came back to me, held up a finger, and said, "It will only be another moment, sir." I made it obvious as I looked at my watch and told the policeman that there didn't seem to be any damage, so perhaps we can just go on our way since we did not want to lose any more of our vacation time. He responded, "Just another moment, sir."

He went back and continued arguing with the man. He shook his hands in the air and slapped his forehead several times. He stopped talking, straightened his jacket once again, and was shaking his head back and forth as he came to me, "Sir, there is a minor problem. Only minor, mind you. I have just given this imbecile a ticket for twenty-five thousand lire (about fourteen dollars). Unfortunately, the fool has only ten thousand lire on him." He closed his eyes, shook his head back and forth, stopped and looked at me plaintively, "Would you be able to lend him fifteen thousand lire?"

I stood there flabbergasted for a moment, then came to my senses. "Yes, of course. Here it is, fifteen thousand lire," I said, noting that this was the only way I would ever leave the scene of the accident.

"Thank you, sir, and don't worry. I will send you a copy of the ticket in the mail. May I suggest that you head back to the main road because the small roads are full of holes and not suitable for such a nice car," he said, regaining his stern composure. He came to his full height, clicked his heels once more, and gave me a brisk salute.

I thanked him and we all got into our cars. I turned our car around and headed back to the state road. I looked in my rearview mirror and saw the two of them arguing with their hands gesticulating wildly. After about five minutes, my wife mentioned that it was a pity we were unable to see the countryside. I thought about it for a moment and said, "Why not? We're on vacation. We probably won't have another chance." And with that, I turned the car around once again.

We drove on and came back to the stop sign, where I stopped once again. We continued to drive past a village called Bertuccia and saw a bar ahead of us on the side of the road. As we cruised by, we spotted the policeman and the fellow who bumped into us sitting at the same table drinking coffee and having a happy conversation. There appeared to be a small glass of grappa in front of each of them.

Needless to say, I never received a copy of that ticket. But I learned to what lengths people will go to enjoy a good cup of coffee—and a good grappa!

THE AUTO ELECTRICIAN

It was mid-September 1994 and I had to deliver a talk at the World Health Organization in Geneva, Switzerland. My wife suggested that we take the week off and drive up from Rome. I thought this would be a good idea, so we made plans to travel through Southern Germany prior to ending up in Geneva. We were scheduled to leave on the weekend, but on Saturday morning the weather throughout the Italian Peninsula and the Alps was terrible, so we decided to leave the following day.

When I went out to the car on Sunday morning, we discovered that it had been broken into the night before and the thieves had cut through most of the wires in their attempt to steal it. Fortunately, the last remaining uncut wires were the ones for the engine ignition and I was able to start the car instantly with my key. Unfortunately, we had no lights, no electrical mirror adjusting, no windshield wipers, and no horn. Since auto electrician places are all closed on Sunday, there was nothing to do but take the short drive to the local Carabinieri station and fill out the report for the insurance.

Monday morning, bright and early, we were waiting

at the front door of our neighborhood *electrauto*. My wife had recently gotten to know this guy quite well since we decided to install a new radio in the car and she had to return no less than four times before it worked properly. The old fellow arrived around 8:15 and was very sympathetic to our dilemma of trying to leave on a short vacation without any electronics in the car. He shook his head in commiseration with us. Putting on his tattered work coat, he looked at me and said, "What a difficult thing it is to start a Monday morning with a job like this." I got the message and immediately ran next door to his bar to get him a caffè, while he and my wife pondered what the world was coming to with all this thievery.

Since his establishment was of the common curbside variety, this meant he had to slide under the car with both his legs sticking out into the street's moving traffic. Miraculously, all the nearby Roman traffic maneuvered around him, leaving both his legs and my fluttering pyloric valve intact. After only ten minutes or so we saw the headlights, taillights, horn, and windshield wipers start to work. He slid out from under the car with a fatigued look on his face. I immediately ran to the bar and brought him back another espresso, which he gratefully accepted, telling me that he was fortunate because his next-door barista used eight grams of coffee instead of the usual seven. He finished the coffee quickly and handed me back the cup. "Would you like another?" I asked. "Later," he replied.

Five minutes later, he was finished and told us it was ready to go. I fetched him another coffee and he said that everything worked, but not quite perfectly—*non e tutto a posto*. He said we might have to make a minor adjustment or two while driving, but it should be fine. The bill he presented to us was very reasonable (sixteen dollars), and he promised to do it all *tutto a posto*, or properly, when we got back from Germany.

We thanked him profusely and jumped into the car, trying to salvage what was left of our mini-vacation. The weather was looking good and the car seemed to be running perfectly. A short while later we were comfortably cruising on the autostrada, headed up toward Austria. I was preparing to pass a very large French twin-trailer rig and gave the customary quick-pull on the high-beam light lever to signal my intention. To my astonishment, instead of engaging the lights, the horn blasted off. I tried it once more and again the horn blared. My wife looked rather annoyed and asked me what I thought I was doing. I tried to explain the situation to her and sounded the horn twice more with the lever to confirm what I had said. Apparently the repeated blasting of the horn was not in our best interests. Reflected in the enormous outside mirror of the rolling leviathan we were passing was the face of one very large, very rough-looking, very, very angry Gaul. I gripped the steering wheel with all the strength I could muster, told my wife to hang on, and bore down on the accelerator, fully prepared for the worst. This proved to be a lifesaving maneuver: the increased momentum allowed us to break through the shockwave that issued from his quadruple-chromed trumpet horns. This experience was as close as I had ever come to levitation—I'm sure the car floated at least four inches off the pavement at the sound of that blast.

I thought of our electrauto and gnashed my teeth. What else might not be *a posto* in the car? We pulled over to the side of the highway and I asked my wife to prepare a list of switches and their corresponding functions. Bright lights = horn; windshield wipers = rear fog light; turn signals = left and right mirrors; rear defrost = interior lights; and so on. I was losing a significant amount of dental enamel but my wife took it all rather calmly, reminding me that the electrauto's bill really was very reasonable. I agreed, silently adding yet another service person to my long list of financial dependents. The French truck driver blasted us again as he sped past.

I wondered if the coffee had anything to do with the way the electrauto reattached the wires.

We decided to stop just short of the Austrian border at the city of Bressanone. This town is an eclectic mix of Gothic, Renaissance, and Baroque architecture and is truly an out-of-the-way gem. The center has tiny streets with lovely covered sidewalks. The main square is dominated by an elegant thirteenth-century twin-spired cathedral in perfect condition. At its side is a cloister containing a courtyard lined with covered walkways. The ceilings are arched in the Gothic style and had been restored to show the hundreds of exquisite paintings of religious and mythical figures. The effect is quite spectacular.

The next morning we carried on to Füssen, the south end of Germany's famous Romantic Road. Our plan was to follow this road all the way to Würtzburg, then head over to the Black Forest and finally on to Geneva. The day was very foggy and the drive uneventful. It was rather cold out so at the first souvenir shop we found, we purchased two heavy felt mountain hats that were typical for the area locals. They were decorated with enamel badges of the various local regions. Just past Füssen, we stopped at a small village called Hohenschwangau, the jumping-off spot to visit the region's beautiful castles. Hohenschwangau was filled with busloads of good-natured, happy Asian tourists photographing everything in sight.

At the hotel we parked the car and walked out into the cool weather, wearing our hats. My wife quickly made her way to the hotel, but I was immediately surrounded by a large group of tourists talking to me in a heavily accented dialect of German-Japanese. I got the impression that they wished to take a picture with me since the hat I was wearing obviously identified me as a local. They were all so enthusiastic, I really couldn't refuse so I said, "*Ja, ja,*" and proceeded to pose for pictures with them. I reluctantly declined the tip they offered me afterward.

The rest of the trip was pretty uneventful with the exception of a near fatal run-in with a cat in the town of Rothenburg ob der Tauber—a stunning and very well-preserved medieval town complete with town walls, moats, pinnacles, turrets, and wonderfully ornate gates. By this time I had gotten used to signaling my turns with the outside mirror switches, turning on the rear fog lamps in order to get the windshield wipers going, and flipping on the interior light to defrost the back window. Unfortunately, I almost killed a cat wandering on the cobblestone street when I forgot about the light lever and flashed him with the brights rather than honking. Fortunately, I deftly swerved the car and neatly avoided the poor beast, which appeared to be in a blind catatonic state as a result of those terrific xenon headlights.

We returned home the following Sunday evening and on Tuesday morning, at 8:15 sharp, I was waiting for the electrauto. I told him the problems we had, but he quickly responded by telling me that he had cautioned us that things were not perfect. In any event, he would make everything right this morning. I nodded my head in satisfaction and he proceeded to don his work coat. I asked him if I could get him a coffee. He accepted with thanks and, with a huge sigh, muttered, "What a way it is to start a Tuesday morning with a job like this!"

Afterword

I t is not the purpose of this book to turn the reader into a botanist, a coffee historian, or a professional taster or a barista, but simply to provide a perspective on coffee's origins, lore, and history, so that coffee can be enjoyed even more. In the course of this voyage we learned of its origins in the Ethiopian Highlands and its journey to the Middle East, Europe, Asia, and the Americas.

From the very first time it was sipped, coffee had a powerful impact upon all mankind and upon our institutions. Without causing us harm, coffee, when consumed in moderation, makes us more alert and able to focus out thoughts and actions. Coffee encourages social interaction at a high intellectual level. This latter property turned out to be both a blessing and a liability for coffee.

The social interaction encouraged by coffee resulted in some of our great institutions and no doubt contributed to generations of creative discussions that led to great discoveries. On the other hand, political leaders feared that such meetings of minds might lead to seditious behavior, which led to the closing down of coffeehouses and the prohibition of consumption on several occasions.

Ultimately, cool heads and logic prevailed, and the enjoyment and the erstwhile benefits were allowed to once again prevail. Although we know that much of coffee's effect is due to its main alkaloid, caffeine, there remains much that we don't know about its other functions. Many other beverages have caffeine, but few stimulate the social interaction or the clarity of mind that coffee does.

Attempts to grow coffee, like so many other valuable commodities that have global markets, were tried in many places, but eventually a few leading producers emerged. Traditional producer regions such as Indonesia, Brazil, and Colombia are supplemented by others like Vietnam, India, Kenya, Central America, the Caribbean, and Hawaii. Most interesting of all, Ethiopia, the ancestral home of coffee, has reentered the market it was responsible for creating more than a thousand years ago.

As times change, so do tastes, and for a time during the twentieth century, our interest in high-quality coffee seemed to decline. Consumers appeared to be more interested in getting *more value* rather than getting *better* coffee. Fortunately, this hiatus of quality did not last long, and toward the end of the twentieth century coffee enjoyed a renaissance.

In fact, coffee's rebirth has had an enormous impact upon us. People can be seen everywhere carrying cups of coffee. We look forward to our coffee whether it is in the morning when we awake, or when we take a short break at work, or when we sip it as a final, relaxing after-dinner beverage—decaffeinated or regular.

The last few years have witnessed great developments in the way coffee is marketed, how it is brewed, and how it is perceived by consumers. I have no doubts that this exciting voyage will continue well into the future.

A Coffee Time Line

*The story of coffee,
from its origins to the present*

c. 700.   Coffee is first extracted by Islamic monks in Ethiopia.

c. 900.   Rhazes, famous Arabian physician, is the first writer to mention coffee, referring to the coffee bean as *bunn* and the extracted drink as *buncham*.

c. 1000.   Avicenna, the most famous of Islamic physicians, is the first writer to explain the medicinal properties of the coffee bean and describes the new drink as "hot and dry and good for the stomach."

c. 1258.   Sheik Omar, disciple of Sheik Schadheli, founder of Mocha, discovers the benefits of coffee as a beverage.

c. 1300.   The coffee drink, made from roasted berries crushed in a mortar with a pestle and placed in boiling water, gains popularity in the region around Mocha.

c. 1350.   The first Persian, Egyptian, and Turkish coffee vessels made of pottery are produced.

c. 1400–
1500.   Perforated metal coffee-roasting plates shaped like skimmers are used in Turkey and Persia in addition to cylindrical bronze coffee mills.

c. 1454.   Sheik Gemaleddin, the mufti of Aden, discovered the benefits of coffee while in Ethiopia and sanctioned its production and use in the fertile region of southwestern and southern Arabia.

1470–
1500.   Coffee consumption spreads to Mecca and Medina.

c. 1505.   The Arabs introduce the coffee plant into Ceylon.

1510.   The coffee is introduced into Cairo, where a large group of Sufi dervishes, originally from Yemen, lived in a cloistered community. It is used to help them remain alert during their prayer services.

1511.   Khayr Beg, governor of Mecca, consults with a council of lawyers, physicians, and politicians and decides to prohibit the use of coffee. In a very short period, this order is revoked by the sultan of Cairo.

1517.   Sultan Selim I brings coffee to Constantinople after conquering Egypt.

1524.   The mufti of Mecca closes the public coffeehouses because of rowdiness but permits coffee drinking at home. However, his replacement relents and allows them to reopen but under government license.

c. 1530.   Coffee drinking introduced into Syria.

1534.   Religious fanatics denounce coffee in Cairo and direct a mob against the coffeehouses, but the chief judge, after consultation with the doctors, permits coffee to continue being served.

1542.   Soliman II takes his turn at trying to prohibit the consumption of coffee but to no avail.

1554.   Constantinople's first coffeehouses open.

c. 1570– Religious zealots in Constantinople claim
1580.   roasted coffee is a form of charcoal and the
         mufti decides that it is forbidden by Islamic
         law. Amurath III orders the closing of all cof-
         feehouses. The order is not strictly observed
         and coffee drinking continues behind closed
         doors. The order is eventually withdrawn.

1573.   Leonhardt Rauwolf, German physician and
         botanist, is the first European documented to
         mention coffee after returning from the
         Levant.

1580.   Prospero Alpini, an Italian physician and
         botanist, goes to Egypt and returns with news
         of coffee.

1582–   First printed reference to coffee is *Rau-*
1583.   *wolf's Travels*, published in German.

1587.   The first authentic account of coffee's origin
         written by Sheik Abd-al-Kadir titled *In Praise
         of Coffee*.

1592.   The first printed description of the coffee
         plant and drink (called *caova*) appears in

Prospero Alpini's work *De Plantis Aegypti liber* (The Plants of Egypt), written in Latin and published in Venice.

1594.   Catholic clerics appeal to Pope Clement VIII to ban coffee. His curiosity piqued, the pope requests that coffee be brought to him in order to make a decision. He is so taken by the beverage's taste and aroma that he immediately blesses it as a truly Christian beverage.

1598.   The first printed reference to coffee in English appears as *Chaona* in a note of Paludanus in *Linschoten's Travels*, translated from the Dutch and published in London.

c. 1600.   Coffee cultivation introduced into southern India at Chickmaglur, Mysore, by a Mecca pilgrim named Baba Budan.

1601.   The first printed reference to coffee in English appears in the book *Sherley's Travels*.

1603.   Captain John Smith, English adventurer and founder of the colony of Virginia, refers in his book *Travels and Adventure* to the Turkish drink *coffa*.

1609.   William Biddulph, a Protestant clergyman who served as a chaplain in Aleppo, Syria, at the turn of the seventeenth century, published his book *The Travels of Certain Englishmen in Africa, Asia, etc. . . .* , describing Turkish coffeehouses.

1610.   The poet Sir George Sandys visits Turkey, Egypt, and Palestine and records that the Turks drink *coffa* in little china dishes as hot as they can tolerate.

1616.   The first coffee is brought from Mocha to Holland by Pieter Van dan Broecke.

1623.   Francis Bacon, in his *Historia Vitae et Mortis* (1623), writes of the Turks' *caphe*, and in his *Sylva Sylvarum* (1627): "They have in Turkey a drink called coffa made of a berry of the same name, as black as soot, and of a strong scent. This drink comforteth the brain and heart, and helpeth digestion."

1628.   William Harvey, insatiable drinker and proponent of coffee, publishes his treatise *An Anatomical Exercise on the Motion of the Heart and Blood in Animals*, the first reliable book on human circulation.

1632.   In his *Anatomy of Melancholy*, Robert Burton says: "The Turks have a drink called coffa, so named from a berry black as soot and as bitter."

1634.   Sir Henry Blount makes a voyage to the Levant and drinks *cauphe* in Turkey.

1637.   Coffee drinking is introduced into England by Nathaniel Canopios, a Cretan student at Balliol College, Oxford.

1640.   The Dutch merchant Wurffbain offers for sale in Amsterdam the first commercial shipment of coffee from Mocha.

1644.   Coffee is introduced into France at Marseilles by P. de la Roque, who brought it back from Constantinople together with appliances for preparing it.

1645.   Venice's first coffeehouse opens.

1650.   England's first coffeehouse is opened in Oxford by a Jew named Jacob.

Coffee is first introduced into Vienna.

1652.   The first London coffeehouse is opened by Pasqua Rosée in St. Michael's Alley, Cornhill.

The first advertisement printed for coffee in English appears as a handbill issued by Pasqua Rosée, acclaiming "The Vertue of the Coffee Drink."

1655.   The Oxford Coffee Club opens and within a short period, some of Oxford's leading scientists, including famed chemist Robert Boyle, regularly gather there to discuss their research and theories. The scientific company of coffee drinkers grows into the world-famous Royal Society.

1656.   Grand Vizier Koprulu suppresses the coffeehouses and prohibits consumption of coffee for political reasons. The punishment for the first violation is cudgeling; for the second, the offender is sewn up in a leather bag and tossed into the Bosporus (the Istanbul Strait).

1657.   The first newspaper advertisement for coffee appears in *The Publick Adviser* of London.

Coffee is introduced privately into Paris by Jean de Thévenot.

1658.   The Dutch start the cultivation of coffee in Ceylon.

1660.   The first French commercial imports of coffee arrive at Marseilles from Egypt.

1663.   All English coffeehouses are required to be licensed.

Regular imports of Mocha coffee begin at Amsterdam.

1665.   Jean de Thévenot, a natural scientist and traveler to the Near East, publishes his book *Relation d'un voyage fait au Levant* (Story of a Journey Made to the Levant), wherein he describes coffee consumed in Turkey.

1668.   Coffee is introduced into North America.

1669.   Coffee is brought into Paris by Soliman Aga, the Turkish ambassador. His lavish receptions feature meals flavored with exotic spices and conclude with Turkish coffee.

1670.   The first attempt to grow coffee in France results in failure.

Coffee is introduced into Germany.

Coffee is first sold in Boston.

1671.   France's first coffeehouse opens.

The first authoritative treatise devoted solely to coffee is written in Latin by the Maronite monk Antonius Faustus Nairon (1635– 1707), professor of theology at the Sorbonne, in his treatise *Discurso sobre a salvberrima bebida chamada cahve, ov café*.

1672.   Pascal, an Armenian, first sells coffee publicly at St.-Germain, Paris, and opens the first Parisian coffeehouse.

1674.   The famous "Women's Petition against Coffee" is published in London.

1675.   Charles II issues a proclamation against sedition and closes all the coffeehouses in London. The order is hastily revoked after pressure from merchants.

1679.   An attempt by the physicians of Marseilles to discredit coffee on dietetic grounds fails and results in a significant increase in consumption.

1683.   Kolschitzky opens Vienna's first coffeehouse, the Blue Bottle.

1684.   Dufour publishes at Lyons, France, the first work on *The Manner of Making Coffee, Tea, and Chocolate.*

1685.   *Café au lait* is first recommended for use as a medicine by Sieur Monin, a celebrated physician of Grenoble, France.

1686.   Germany's first coffeehouse opens in Regensburg.

1689.   Café le Procope, the first authentic French café, is opened in Paris by François Procope of Florence.

Boston's first coffeehouse opens.

1696.   New York's first coffeehouse, the King's Arms, opens.

1696.   Coffee seedlings are brought from Kananur on the Malabar coast and introduced into Java near Batavia (Jakarta) for the first time. They are soon destroyed by flood.

1699.   Coffee plants from the second shipment from Malabar to Java become the progenitors of all the arabica coffee trees in the Dutch East Indies.

1700.   Philadelphia's first coffeehouse opens.

1706.   The first samples of Java coffee, along with a live coffee plant, are received at Amsterdam's botanical gardens.

1711.   Java coffee is first sold at public auction in Amsterdam.

A novelty in coffee making is introduced in France: infusing ground beans in a linen bag.

1714.   A coffee plant, raised from the seed of the plant received at Amsterdam's botanical gardens in 1706, is presented to Louis XIV of France. It is nurtured in the Jardin des Plantes, Paris.

1715.   Coffee cultivation is introduced into Haiti and Santo Domingo.

1717.   Johann Hübner's famous German encyclopedia, *Curieuses und reales Natur- Kunst-*

Berg- Gewerck- und Handlungs-Lexicon, repeats the story of Khaldi and his dancing goats.

1718.   Coffee cultivation is introduced into Surinam by the Dutch.

1720.   Caffè Florian is opened in Venice by Floriano Francesconi.

1723.   Gabriel de Clieu, a French captain of infantry, sails from France, accompanied by one of the seedlings presented to Louis XIV. He shares his drinking water with it to ensure its survival during a protracted voyage to Martinique.

1730.   The English bring the cultivation of coffee to Jamaica.

1732.   Bach's celebrated "Coffee Cantata" is published in Leipzig.

1737.   The Merchants' Coffeehouse is established in New York and is called the true cradle of American liberty and the birthplace of the Union.

1747.   The genus *Coffea* was first described by Carolus Linnaeus in a poetic account describing how it induces insomnia, makes the hands tremble, and causes strokes to those who drink it.

1752.   Intensive coffee cultivation is reintroduced in the Portuguese colonies in Brazil.

1760.   In France, the boiling of coffee is replaced by the infusion method.

1761.   Carolus Linnaeus produces a botanical and medical history of the coffee tree and its fruits, concluding that coffee destroys the appetite, promotes flatulence, and is noxious to depressed, hypochondriacal, and hysterical people.

1763.   A tinsmith of St. Benoit, France, invents a new coffeepot with a tap to draw coffee. Inside is a flannel sack to prepare the coffee infusion.

1777.   King Frederick the Great of Prussia issues his coffee and beer manifesto, urging the greater consumption of beer.

1781.   King Frederick the Great of Prussia establishes state control over coffee roasting in Germany and makes it a government monopoly. Citizens are forbidden to roast coffee and are under the constant surveillance of inspectors sniffing around for coffee.

1784.   A prohibition against the use of coffee is promulgated by Maximilian Frederick, elector of Cologne. The rich are exempt from this rule.

1790.   Coffee is introduced into Mexico from the West Indies.

The first US advertisement for coffee appears in the *New York Daily Advertiser*.

The first prepackaged coffee is sold in stoneware pots and jars in New York.

1792.   The Tontine coffeehouse is established in New York.

c. 1804.   The first American cargo of coffee from Mocha arrives in Salem, Massachusetts.

1806.   The first French patent on an improved French drip coffeepot is granted.

The coffee percolator is invented by Count Rumford (Benjamin Thompson), an expatriate American scientist in Paris.

1809.   The first coffee imported from Brazil by the United States arrives at Salem, Massachusetts.

c. 1817.   The coffee biggin (said to have been invented by a man named Biggin) comes into common use in England.

1819.   Friedlieb Ferdinand Runge first extracts and purifies caffeine from coffee beans as a result of an encounter with Goethe.

Laurens is granted a French patent on the original pumping-percolator device in which the boiling water is raised by steam pressure and sprayed over the ground coffee.

1820.   Another early form of the French percolator is patented by Gaudet, a Paris tinsmith.

1825.   The first coffeepot patent in the United States is issued to Lewis Martelley in New York.

Coffee cultivation is brought into Hawaii from Rio de Janeiro.

1832.   Government coffee cultivation by forced labor is introduced into Java.

1840.   Central America begins shipping coffee to the United States.

c. 1840.   Robert Napier of England invents the Napierian vacuum coffee machine to make coffee by distillation and filtration.

1842.   The first French patent on a glass coffee-making device is granted to Mme. Vassieux of Lyons.

c. 1850.   The cultivation of coffee is introduced into Guatemala.

c. 1860.   Osborn's Celebrated Prepared Java Coffee, the first packaged ground-roasted coffee, is put on the New York market by Lewis A. Osborn.

1864.   Jabez Burns of New York is granted a US patent for the Burns coffee roaster, the first roaster that did not have to be moved away from the fire for discharging roasted coffee. This marks a distinct advance in the manufacture of coffee-roasting apparatuses.

1865.   In Pittsburgh John Arbuckle introduces roasted coffee in individual packages, the forerunner of the Ariosa package.

1867.   Jabez Burns is granted US patents for a coffee cooler, a coffee mixer, and a grinding mill, or granulator.

1868.   John Arbuckle is granted a US patent for a roasted-coffee coating consisting of Irish moss, isinglass, gelatin, sugar, and eggs.

1870.   Thos. Smith & Son of Glasgow, Scotland, begins the manufacture of the Napierian vacuum coffee-making machines for brewing coffee.

1872.   Jabez Burns is granted a US patent on an improved coffee-granulating mill.

Robert Hewitt Jr. of New York publishes the first American work on coffee, *Coffee: Its History, Cultivation, and Uses.*

1873.   Ariosa, first successful national brand of package coffee, is put on the US market by John Arbuckle of Pittsburgh.

1878.   Boston coffee roasters Chase and Sanborn are the first to package and ship roasted coffee in sealed containers.

1880.   Henry E. Smyser of Philadelphia is granted a US patent on a package making-and-filling machine, a forerunner of the weighing-and-packing machine.

1881.   Jabez Burns is granted a US patent on an improved construction of roaster, comprising a front head that serves for both feeding and discharging.

Francis B. Thurber of New York publishes the second important American work on coffee, *Coffee from Plantation to Cup*.

1894.   A small company called Murchie's opens its doors in Vancouver in order to import quality teas and the best arabica coffee.

1898.   The Hobart Manufacturing Co. of Troy, Ohio, puts one of the first coffee grinders connected with an electric motor on the market. Hobart eventually forms KitchenAid Products.

1899.   Soluble coffee is invented in Chicago by Dr. Satori Kato, a chemist of Tokyo.

1900.   Hills Brothers of San Francisco is the first to vacuum pack coffee under the Norton patents.

1901.   Kato's soluble coffee is put on the United States market by the Kato Coffee Company.

         American Can Co. begins the manufacture and sale of tin coffee cans in the United States.

1902.   Robusta coffee is introduced into Java.

1903.   A US patent on a coffee concentrate and process of making the same (soluble coffee) is granted to Satori Kato of Chicago, assignor to the Kato Coffee Company of Chicago.

1905.   H. L. Johnston is granted a US patent on a coffee mill that he assigns to the Hobart Manufacturing Co. of Troy, Ohio.

1907.   Desiderio Pavoni of Milan is granted a patent in Italy for an improvement on the Bezzara system of preparing and serving coffee as a rapid infusion of a single cup.

1908.   German housewife Melitta Bentz invents the paper filter coffeemaker.

1910.   German caffeine-free coffee is first introduced to the trade of the United States by Merck & Co., New York, under the brand name Dekafa, later changed to Dekofa.

1912.   The Maillard reaction was first discovered by the French chemist Louis Camille Maillard. He is the first to characterize the reaction that occurs between sugars and proteins when they are heated together—a reaction that is responsible for most of the changes in color and flavor that take place when foods are cooked.

1914.   The Kaffee Hag Corporation is organized in New York to continue marketing the German caffeine-free coffee under its original German brand name in the United States.

1918.   The original soluble coffee company Kato started is organized into the Soluble Coffee Company of America to supply this type of soluble coffee to the American army overseas.

1933. Together, Standard Brands and General Foods spend almost 3 million dollars on radio ads for coffee.

1955. Alfred Peet moves to San Francisco, bringing his coffee and tea experience to E. A. Johnson & Co., importers of coffee.

1966. On April Fool's Day, Alfred Peet opens Peet's Coffee and Tea Inc. on the corner of Walnut and Vine streets in Berkeley, California, initiating the renaissance of coffee in America.

1971. Vincent Marotta, Edward Able, and Erwin Schulze develop the Mr. Coffee machine.

Seattle writer Gordon Bowker and his friends Jerry Baldwin and Zev Siegl each invest $1,350 and borrow another $5,000 from the bank in order to open their first Seattle store in Pike Place Market. They choose the name Starbucks in honor of Starbuck, the first mate on the whaling ship *Pequod* under the command of Captain Ahab in Herman Melville's *Moby Dick*.

1972. The second Starbucks store is opened in Seattle after the first exceeds all expectations.

1982.   After a visit to Seattle and discussion with owners, Howard Schultz takes on the responsibility of marketing for Starbucks.

1983.   Schultz gets an epiphany while visiting Italy to attend a trade show. He decides to bring the Italian bar experience to America.

1986.   Schultz opens up his first coffee bar under the name of Il Giornale in April 1986, starting a trend.

1987.   Howard Schultz and his board of directors agree to buy Starbucks when it comes up for sale and complete the deal in August. At the age of thirty-four, Schultz becomes the president and CEO of Starbucks Corporation.

1992.   Starbucks goes public with their initial IPO in June. It is enormously successful and the injection of capital greatly accelerates their expansion of store operations.

2006.   Dunkin' Donuts starts an ad campaign to revolutionize the brand's standing by focusing on how Dunkin' Donuts keeps busy Americans fueled and on the go.

2008.   Starbucks has more than fifteen thousand
            stores, joint ventures, and licensed operations
            around the world. Starbucks is no longer an
            American phenomenon; it is a world wonder.

Endnotes

PROLOGUE

1. C. M. Villanueva, K. P. Cantor, W. D. King, J. J. K. Jaakkola, S. Cordier, C. F. Lynch, S. Porru, and M. Kogevinas, "Total and Specific Fluid Consumption as Determinants of Bladder Cancer Risk," *International Journal of Cancer* 118, no. 8 (2006): 2040–47.

CHAPTER 1

1. J. R. Harlan, "Indigenous African Agriculture," in *Agricultural Origins in World Perspective*, ed. P. J. Watson and C. W. Cowan (Washington, DC: Smithsonian Institution Publications in Anthropology, 1992), pp. 59–70.

2. Food for the Hungry International, "Christian History: Christianity in Ethiopia," http://www.fhi.net/fhius/ethiopia famine/christian.html (accessed March 22, 2008).

3. "The Table," Koran, chapter 5, sura 90.

4. B. G. Gardiner, "The Linnaean Tercentenary, Some Aspects of Linnaeus' Life—Linnaeus' Medical Career," http://www.linnean.org/fileadmin/images/The_Linnean_-_Tercentenary/2-Medical_career.pdf (accessed February 11, 2008).

5. J. A. Gomez-Ruiz, J. M. Ames, and D. S. Leake, "Antioxidant Activity and Protective Effects of Green and Dark Coffee Components against Human Low-Density Lipoprotein Oxidation," *European Food Research and Technology* 227 (2008): 1017–24.

6. International Coffee Organization, "Field Processing," http://www.ico.org/field_processing.asp (accessed February 9, 2008).

7. "Cure for Coffee," *Time*, http://www.time.com/time/magazine/article/0,9171,902015,00.html (accessed May 5, 2008).

CHAPTER 2

1. R. J. Clarke and R. Macrae, eds., *Coffee, Volume I—Chemistry* (London: Elsevier Applied Science, 1985).

2. S. L. Rovner, "Tweaking Coffee's Flavor Chemistry—Roasting, Cooling, and Storage Conditions Affect the Chemicals That Contribute to Brew's Flavor and Aroma," *Chemical & Engineering News* 85, no. 38 (September 17, 2007).

3. L. C. Amstalden, F. Leite, and H. Menezes, "Identification and Quantification of Coffee Volatile Components through High Resolution Gas Chromatoghaph/Mass Spectrometer Using a Headspace Automatic Sampler," *Ciência e Tecnologia de Alimentos* 21, no. 1 (2001): 123–28.

4. A. S. Blumgarten, *Textbook of Materia Medica*, 4th ed. (New York: MacMillan, 1927), p. 286.

5. International Food Information Council Foundation, "Fact Sheet: Caffeine and Health," August 2007, http://ific .org/publications/factsheets/upload/Caffeine-and-Health -formatted.pdf (accessed May 3, 2008).

6. Ibid.

7. K. Ritchie, I. Carrière, A. de Mendonca, F. Portet, J. F. Dartigues, O. Rouaud, P. Barberger-Gateau, and M. L. Ancelin, "The Neuroprotective Effects of Caffeine," *Neurology* 69 (2007): 536–45.

8. American Psychiatric Association, *Diagnostic and Statistical Manual of Mental Disorders* (Arlington, VA: American Psychiatric Press, 1994).

9. Health Canada, "Caffeine and Your Health," http:// www.hc-sc.gc.ca/fn-an/securit/facts-faits/caffeine-eng.php (accessed May 12, 2008).

10. Jerry M. Rice, "Carcinogens in Coffee," Winter Toxicology Forum, Washington, DC, 2005.

11. P. Nawrot, S. Jordan, J. Eastwood, J. Rotstein, A. Hugenholtz, and M. Feeley, "Effects of Caffeine on Human Health," *Food Additives and Contaminants* 20, no. 1 (2003): 1–30.

12. A. Tavani and C. La Vecchia, "Coffee, Decaffeinated Coffee, Tea and Cancer of the Colon and Rectum: A Review of Epidemiological Studies, 1990–2003," *Cancer Causes Control* 8 (2004): 743–57.

13. P. J. Boekema, M. Samsom, and A. J. Smout, "Effect of Coffee on Gastro-Oesophageal Reflux in Patients with Reflux Disease and Healthy Controls," *European Journal of Gastroenterology and Hepatology* 11, no. 11 (1999): 1271–76.

14. T. Kaltenbach, S. Crockett, and L. B. Gerson, "Are Lifestyle Measures Effective in Patients with Gastroesophageal Reflux Disease? An Evidence-Based Approach," *Archives of Internal Medicine* 166 (2006): 965–71.

15. A. P. Smith, "Caffeine at Work," *Human Psychopharmacology* 20, no. 6 (2005): 441–45.

16. A. Leviton and L. Cowan, "A Review of the Literature Relating Caffeine Consumption by Women to Their Risk of Reproductive Hazards," *Food and Chemical Toxicology* 40, no. 9 (2002): 1271–1310.

17. International Food Information Council Foundation and Association of Women's Health, Obstetric, and Neonatal Nurses, "Caffeine and Women's Health," August 2002, http://www.ific.org/publications/brochures/upload/Caffeine -and-Women-s-Health.pdf (accessed May 3, 2008).

18. Ibid.

19. Ibid.

20. Ibid.

21. Mogens Vestergaard, Kirsten Wisborg, Tine Brink Henriksen, Niels Jørgen Secher, John R. Østergaard, and Jørn Olsen, "Prenatal Exposure to Cigarettes, Alcohol, and Coffee and the Risk for Febrile Seizures," *Pediatrics* 116, no. 5 (2005): 1089–94; American Academy of Pediatrics Committee on Drugs, "Policy Statement: The Transfer of Drugs and Other Chemicals into Human Milk," *Pediatrics* 108, no. 3 (2001): 776–89.

22. E. Salazar-Martinez, W. C. Willett, A. Ascherio, J. E. Manson, M. F. Leitzmann, M. J. Stampfer, and F. B. Hu, "Coffee Consumption and Risk for Type 2 Diabetes Mellitus," *Annals of Internal Medicine* 140, no. 1 (2004): 1–8.

23. Esther Lopez-Garcia, Rob M. van Dam, Tricia Y. Li, Fernando Rodriguez-Artalejo, and Frank B. Hu, "The Rela-

tionship of Coffee Consumption with Mortality," *Annals of Internal Medicine* 148, no. 12 (2008): 904–14.

24. R. R. Knipling and J. S. Wang, "Crashes and Fatalities Related to Driver Drowsiness/Fatigue," research note, US Department of Transportation, Office of Crash Avoidance Research, Washington, DC, 1994.

25. J. A. Horne and L. A. Reyner, "Vehicle Accidents Related to Sleep: A Review," *Occupational and Environmental Medicine* 56 (1999): 289–94.

26. G. Defazio, D. Martino, et al., "Influence of Coffee Drinking and Cigarette Smoking on the Risk of Primary Late Onset Blepharospasm: Evidence from a Multicentre Case Control Study," *Journal of Neurology, Neurosurgery, and Psychiatry* 78 (2007): 877–79.

27. S. Norr, "The Healthy Benefits of Our Beloved Nectar," *Tea and Coffee Trade Online* 178, no. 10 (October/November 2006), http://www.teaandcoffee.net/1006/coffee.htm (accessed May 3, 2008).

CHAPTER 3

1. William H. Ukers, *All about Coffee* (New York: Tea and Coffee Trade Journal Company, 1922), p. 12.

2. J. Sweetman, *The Oriental Obsession: Islamic Inspiration in British and American Art* (Cambridge: Cambridge University Press, 1987), pp. 72–85.

3. Ukers, *All about Coffee*, p. 14.

4. John Ellis, *An Historical Account of Coffee with an Engraving, and Botanical Description of the Tree* (London: printed for Edward and Charles Dilly, 1774).

5. J. J. Scheuzer, *Physique Sacreé ou Histoire Naturelle de la Bible* (Amsterdam: 1732), p. 329.

6. K. Niebuhr, *Descriptions of Arabia*, translated by Heron (Amsterdam: 1774), p. 266.

7. T. Houtsma, A. J. Wensinck, and H. A. R. Gibb, eds., *The Encyclopædia of Islam: A Dictionary of the Geography, Ethnography and Biography of the Muhammadan Peoples*, vol. 4 (1934).

CHAPTER 4

1. L. Rauwolf, *Aigentliche Beschreibung der Raiss, so er von Diser zeit Gegen Auffgang inn die Morgenlander, Furnemlich Syriam, Iudaeam, Arabiam, Mesopotamiam, Babyloniam, Assyriam, Armeniam &c,*" (Itinerary into the Eastern Countries: Syria, Palestine, Armenia, Mesopotamia, etc.) (Selbs Volbracht, 1582).

2. Jean de Thévenot, *Relation d'un voyage fait au Levant* (Paris: 1665).

3. John Aubrey, *Brief Lives, Chiefly of Contemporaries Set Down by John Aubrey, between the Years 1669 & 1696*, edited from the author's manuscript by Andrew Clark (Oxford: Clarendon Press, 1898), p. 301.

4. Anthony Wood, *Athenae Oxonienses: An Exact History of All the Writer's and Bishops Who Have Had Their Education in the Most Ancient and Famous University of Oxford from the Fifteenth Year of King Henry Seventh Dom. 1500 to the End the Year 1690* (London: 1692).

CHAPTER 5

1. *Union Text Book* (Philadelphia: G. G. Evans, 1860), p. 193.

2. Joel Schapira, *The Book of Coffee and Tea: A Guide to the Appreciation of Fine Coffees* (New York: Macmillan, 1996), p. 13.

CHAPTER 6

1. Pramoedya Ananta Toer, "The Book That Killed Colonialism," *New York Times Magazine*, April 18, 1999, pp. 112–14.

2. D. P. Kidder and J. C. Fletcher, *Brazil and the Brazilians* (Philadelphia: Childs & Peterson, Philadelpha, 1857), p. 438.

3. Ibid., p. 132.

4. A. Nicholls and C. Opal, *Fair Trade: Market-Driven Ethical Consumption* (London: Sage Publications, 2004).

CHAPTER 7

1. "Researching Historic Buildings in the British Isles, Part II: Coffee-Houses of Old London," http://www.building history.org/Primary/Inns/Coffee1.htm (accessed April 17, 2008).

2. William H. Ukers, *All about Coffee* (New York: Tea and Coffee Trade Journal Company, 1922), p. 56.

3. John Milton, *The Ready and Easy Way to Establish a*

Free Commonwealth, edited with introduction, notes, and glossary by Evert Mordecai Clark (New Haven, CT: Yale University Press, 1915), ch. 2, "The Rota Club," http://oll.liberty fund.org/title/272/41712 on 2008-04-17 (accessed April 17, 2008).

4. *The Diary of Samuel Pepys*, edited by H. B. Wheatley (London: George Bell and Sons, 1893).

5. W. Carew Hazlitt, *The Venetian Republic, Its Rise, Its Growth, and Its Fall: 421–1797, Volume II* (London: Adam and Charles Black, 1900), p. 792.

6. M. le Chevallier de Mailly, *Les Entreriens des Cafés de Paris et les differens qui y surviement, par A. Trévault chez Etienne Ganeau* (1702).

CHAPTER 8

1. S. Ataka, M. Tanaka, S. Nozaki, H. Mizuma, K. Mizuno, T. Tahara, T. Sugino, T. Shirai, Y. Kajimoto, H. Kuratsune, O. Kajimoto, and Y. Watanabe, "Effects of Oral Administration of Caffeine and D-Ribose on Mental Fatigue," *Nutrition* 24, no. 3 (2008): 233–38.

CHAPTER 10

1. "Kopi Luwak," Wikipedia, http://en.wikipedia.org/wiki/Kopi_Luwak (accessed April 20, 2008).

2. Tom Chivers, "Cat Dung Coffee, on Sale Now at Just £50 a Cup," *(London) Telegraph*, April 9, 2008, http://

www.telegraph.co.uk/news/main.jhtml?xml=/news/2008/04/09/ncoffee109.xml (accessed April 20, 2008).

3. Food and Agricultural Organization of United Nations: Economic and Social Department: The Statistical Division (accessed May 20, 2008).

4. Ibid.

5. Euromonitor International, Global Market Information Database.

6. Food and Agricultural Organization of United Nations: Economic and Social Department: The Statistical Division.

7. K. Cornel, "Hamburg's Harbor—Main Thoroughfare for Coffee and Tea," *Tea & Coffee Trade Journal* (June 1, 1990): 37.

8. T. J. Castle, "Instant Is Coffee, Too!" *Tea and Coffee Trade Online*, http://www.teaandcoffee.net/1001/special.htm (accessed May 22, 2008).

9. Han-Seok Seo, Misato Hirano, Junko Shibato, Randeep Rakwal, Kyeong Hwang, and Yoshinori Masuo, "Effects of Coffee Bean Aroma on the Rat Brain Stressed by Sleep Deprivation: A Selected Transcript and 2D Gel-Based Proteome Analysis," *Journal of Agricultural and Food Chemicals* 56 (2008): 4665–73.

CHAPTER 12

1. J. Grierson, "History of the Cafetiere," EzineArticles, 2008, http://ezinearticles.com/?History-of-the-Cafetiere&id=152825 (accessed May 4, 2008).

2. Many thanks for this reference to Brian Harris, whose

superb Web page, "Vacuum Coffee Pots," is unlike any other on the Internet. It can be viewed at http://baharris.org/coffee/VacuumCoffeePots.htm.

CHAPTER 13

1. World Barista Championship, "WBC Rules and Regulations Version: VIII," p. 4, http://www.worldbaristachampionship.com/pdf/WBC_Rules_and_Regulations.pdf (accessed May 14, 2008).

2. T. Wendelboe, "The Future of the World Barista Championship," Viva Barista, http://vivabarista.com/content/view/107/39/ (accessed May 14, 2008).

Select Bibliography

Allen, Stewart L. *The Devil's Cup: A History of World according to Coffee*. New York: Ballantine Books, 1999.

Anonymous. *Coffee*. New York: Pan American Coffee Bureau, 1947.

Davids, Kenneth. *Espresso: Ultimate Coffee*. New York: St. Martin's Griffin, 2001.

Hattox, Ralph S. *Coffee and Coffeehouses*. Seattle: University of Washington Press, 1985.

Jacob, Heinrich E. *Coffee: The Epic of a Commodity*. New York: Viking, 1935.

Luttinger, Nina, and Gregory Dicum. *The Coffee Book: Anatomy of an Industry from Crop to the Last Drop*. New York: New Press, 2006.

Michelli, Joseph. *The Starbucks Experience: 5 Principles for Turning Ordinary into Extraordinary*. New York: McGraw-Hill, 2007.

Pendergrast, Mark. *Uncommon Grounds*. New York: Basic Books, 1999.

Rolnick, Harry. *The Complete Book of Coffee*. Hong Kong: Rolf Stacker, 1982.

Schapira, Joel. *The Book of Coffee and Tea: A Guide to the Appreciation of Fine Coffees*. New York: Macmillan, 1996.

Ukers, William H. *All about Coffee*. New York: Tea and Coffee Trade Journal Company, 1922.

Weinberg, B. A., and B. K. Bealer. *The World of Caffeine*. New York: Routledge, 2001.

Wild, Anthony. *Coffee: A Dark History*. New York: W. W. Norton, 2004.

Young, Isabel N. *The Story of Coffee*. New York: Bureau of Coffee Information, 1931.

Index